The Outdoor Girls in the Saddle

BY

LAURA LEE HOPE

[ZHINGOORA BOOKS]

This edition is published by
Zhingoora Books.

The Cover is Designed by Pallav Sethiya.

CONTENTS

chapter

CHAPTER I

A SUMMER IN THE SADDLE

"Hello, hello! Oh, what is the matter with central!"

The dark-haired, pink-cheeked girl at the telephone jiggled the receiver impatiently while a straight line of impatience marred her pretty mouth.

"Oh dear, oh dear!"

"At last! Is that you, Mollie Billette? I've been trying to get you for the last half hour. What's that? You've been home all morning twiddling your thumbs and wondering what to do with yourself? Of course! I knew it was central's fault all the time! Now listen! Goodness, what are you having over at your house? A jazz dance or something? I can hardly hear you speak for the noise."

"No, it isn't a dance," came back Mollie's voice wearily from the other end of the wire. "It's just the twins. They want to talk to you. Hold the wire a minute while I shut them in the other room."

Followed a silence during which Betty Nelson could distinctly hear the wails of Mollie's little brother and sister as they were ushered forcibly into an adjoining room. Then Mollie's voice again at the phone.

"Hello," she said. "Still there, Betty? Guess I can hear you a little better now. Mother's out, and I've been taking care of the twins. Just rescued the cat from being dumped head down in the flour barrel."

"Sounds natural," laughed the dark-haired, pink-cheeked one, as she visualized Mollie's little brother and sister, Dodo and Paul. They were twins, and always in trouble.

"Anything special you called up about?" asked Mollie's voice from the other end of the wire. "Want to go for a ride or something?"

"Not the kind of ride you mean," said the brown-eyed, pink-cheeked one, with a knowing little smile on her lips.

At the lilt in her voice Mollie, at her end of the wire, sat up and stared inquiringly into the black mouth of the telephone.

"Betty," she said hopefully, "you are hidingsomething from me. You have something up your sleeve."

"You're right and wrong," giggled Betty. "I'm hiding something from you, but I can't get it up my sleeve, it's too big!"

"Hurry up!" commanded Mollie in terrific accents. "Are you going to tell me what's on your mind, Betty Nelson?"

"When will you be around?" countered Betty.

"In five minutes."

"Good!"

"Betty, wait! Is it good news?"

"The best ever," and Betty rang off.

She twinkled at the telephone for a minute, then called another number.

"That you, Gracie?"

The fair-haired, tall, and very graceful girl at the other end of the wire acknowledged that it was.

"Please suggest something interesting, Betty," she added plaintively, as she took a chocolate from the ever-present candy box and nibbled on it discontentedly. "I woke up with the most awful attack of the blues this morning."

"What, with a whole summer full of blessed idleness before you?" mocked Betty.

"Too much idleness," grumbled Grace. "That's the trouble."

Grace digested this remark for a moment, staring at the telephone in much the same manner as Mollie had done a few minutes before. Then she swallowed the last of her chocolate in such haste that it almost choked her.

"Betty," she said, "I have heard you use that tone before. Is there really something in the wind?"

"Come and see," said Betty and a click at the other end of the wire told Grace that the conversation was over.

"Oh bother!" she cried, her pretty forehead drawn into a frown. "Now I suppose I've got to get dressed and go over there before I can find out what she meant."

In the hall she nearly ran into her mother, who was dressed to go out. Mrs. Ford was a handsome woman, prominent in the social circles of Deepdale. She was kindly and sympathetic, and all who knew her loved her.

So now, as she regarded her mother, a loving smile erased the frown from Grace's forehead.

"I declare, Mother, you look younger than I do," she said fondly. "Whither away so early?"

"The art club, this morning," replied Mrs. Ford, her eyes approving the fair prettiness odff her daughter. "Are you going out? I thought you were deep in that new book."

"I was," said Grace, with a sigh for what might have been. "But Betty called up and said she wanted me to come over. There's something in the wind, that's sure, but she wouldn't give me even the teeniest little hint of what it was. I wasn't going at first, but I——"

"Thought better of it," finished Mrs. Ford, with a smile. "Better go," she added, as she opened the door. "My experience with Betty Nelson is that she usually has something interesting to say. Good-by, dear. If any one should 'phone while you are here, will you tell them that I shan't be back till late afternoon?"

Grace promised that she would and moved slowly up the stairs.

Meanwhile Amy Blackford, the last of the trio to whom the dark-haired, pink-cheeked little person who was Betty Nelson had telephoned, had stopped merely to remove the apron from in front of her pink-checked gingham dress and was now flying along the two short blocks that separated her house from the Nelsons'.

As for poor Mollie Billette, she was nearly distracted. Torn with curiosity, as that young person very often was, to know the facts that had prompted Betty's early call, she yet could not satisfy that curiosity. When she had told Betty that she would be around in five minutes she had fully meant to make that promise good. But—she had forgotten the twins!

Upon entering the room where she had locked them while she talked to Betty, she found a sight that fairly took her breath away.

Unfortunately, some one had left an open bottle of ink on the table. One of the twins, deciding to play "savages," had pounced upon the ink bottle as a means of making the play more realistic!

"Oh, Dodo! Oh, Paul! How could you be so naughty?" moaned Mollie, sinking to the floor, while the tears of exasperation rolled down her face.

"Paul did it," accused Dodo, waving a pudgy, ink-stained little fist in the direction of her brother. "He said, 'let's use this ink and play we're savagers——'"

It was upon this scene that Mollie's little French-American mother, Mrs. Billette, came a moment later.

"Oh! Oh!" she cried, raising her hands in the French gesture all French people know so well. "What is this? Mollie, have you gone quite mad?"

Whereupon Mollie shook the tears of woe from her eyes and explained to her mother just what had happened.

"And I was in such a hurry to get to Betty's," she finished dismally. "I just know she has something exciting to tell us. And now I don't suppose I will get there for hours."

"Oh yes, you will," said Mrs. Billette, with the delicious, almost imperceptible, accent she had. "The ink has not yet dried, and luckily there is not much about the room. Run along, dear. I fully realize," she added, with the smile that made Mollie adore her, "that this, with you, is a very important occasion."

"And you are the most precious mother in the world!" cried Mollie, flinging young arms about her mother and giving her a joyful hug. "I might have known you would understand." And before the words were fairly out of her mouth she was flying up the stairs.

When she reached Betty's house at last, out of breath but happy, she found that Grace and Amy were there before her. She found them all, including Betty, up in Betty's room, a pretty place done in ivory and blue, awaiting her coming as patiently as they could.

"Betty wouldn't tell us a thing until you came," was the greeting Grace flung at her.

"So don't be surprised if you aren't very popular around here," laughed Betty, sitting very straight in her wicker chair, feet stretched out and crossed in front of her, hands tightly clasped in her lap. Her face was a pretty picture of animation.

"Who cares for popularity?" cried Mollie, as she flung her sport hat on the bed and turned to face Betty. "Betty Nelson, bring out that surprise."

"Who said it was a surprise?" asked Betty tantalizingly, but the next minute her face sobered and she regarded the girls gravely.

"Girls," she said, "I think I see a chance for the most glorious outing we have had yet. How would you like——" she paused and regarded the expectant girls thoughtfully. "How would you like a summer *in the saddle?*"

"In the saddle?" repeated Grace wonderingly, but Mollie broke in with a quick:

"Betty, do you mean on horseback?"

"Real horses?" breathed Amy Blackford.

"Yes," said Betty, nodding. "That's just exactly what I mean."

CHAPTER II

GREAT HOPES

"But where are we to do all this?" asked Grace skeptically. "Is somebody giving away steeds for the asking? Wake me up, somebody, when Betty gets through dreaming."

"Keep still, you old wet blanket," cried Mollie. "Can't you see Betty is really in earnest?"

"Never mind them," said Amy, leaning a little breathlessly toward Betty. "Let them fight it out between themselves. What is the great news, Betty?"

"It is great news," said Betty radiantly. "Listen, my children. Mother has received a legacy from a great uncle that she had almost forgotten she had."

"Money?" queried Grace, interested.

"No, that's the best part of it," said Betty. "Oh, girls, it's a ranch, a great big beautiful ranch in the really, truly west!"

"Honest-to-goodness, wild and woolly?" queried Mollie, beaming.

"Better than that," answered Betty with the same lilt to her voice that the girls had heard over the telephone. "I shouldn't wonder if we should find the real old-fashioned, movie kind of cowboys there—sombreros, fur leggings, bandannas, and all."

"But where," interrupted Mollie, who had been waiting with more or less patience for Betty to come to the point, "do we come in, in all this? I fail to see——"

"Oh hush," cried Betty, her eyes dancing. "You interrupt entirely too much. Where do we come in, she wants to know," she paused to bestow a beaming glance on Grace and Amy. "That's the biggest joke of all. Where do we come in? Why, honey dear, we're the whole show!"

"The whole show," they murmured, beginning to see the light.

"You bet," said the brown-haired, rosy-cheeked one slangily. "Now listen. I think I've about argued mother and dad around to the point where they'll agree to let us have the use of this wild and woolly rancho for a real outdoor adventure. How does that idea strike you?"

"Listen to the child," cried Mollie pityingly. "Such a question!"

"It would be heavenly!" raved Grace. "Think of riding around all day in fur leggings and a sombrero. Wide hats are always becoming to me," she added musingly.

The girls laughed and Betty threw a pillow at her, missing her by a hair's breadth.

"You needn't worry about your hat," laughed Betty. "Reckon there won't be anybody around there to admire you but Indians and broncho busters."

"Oh, aren't the boys coming?" Grace asked, her disappointment in her voice.

"They haven't been asked, silly," Mollie interrupted impatiently. "Tell me, Betty," she cried, turning to the Little Captain. "Is it really certain that we'll have this chance?"

"No, it isn't," admitted Betty, her bright face sobering. "That's why I don't want you to get too excited about it. You see," her voice lowered confidentially, "dad might decide to sell it."

"Sell it!" they cried in dismay, and Grace added, with a decision that made the girls laugh:

"Oh, he mustn't do that until the fall, anyway."

"All right, Gracie," said Betty, with a chuckle. "I'll give dad his orders."

"But why does he want to sell it, Betty?" Amy questioned.

"We-el," said the Little Captain slowly. "You see mother has already received an offer of fifteen thousand dollars for it. There's a ranchman out there, I think his name is John Josephs, or some such name, who seems to want to get hold of our ranch. So his lawyers have offered mother fifteen thousand for it."

"That's a pretty good lot of money," said Amy thoughtfully.

"Yes, it is," agreed Betty. "And dad seems to think that the best thing mother could do would be to take the money and get rid of the ranch. He says it will be a sort of white elephant on our hands, since there isn't very much chance of our going out there to live," she ended, with a chuckle.

"Well," said Grace, with an injured air, "I don't see why you called us all over here just to disappoint us. If your father is going to sell the place, then we certainly sha'n't be able to make ourselves beautiful with bandannas and picturesque hats——"

"Ah, but you did not let me finish," hissed Betty, melodramatically. "We have one ally—my mother."

"Your mother!" cried Mollie, eagerly. "Then she doesn't want to sell the ranch?"

"Right, the first time," cried Betty hilariously. "I think mother has a sneaking notion that she might look pretty good in a cowboy make-up herself. You see," she added, with a twinkle, "mother has never had a chance to own a real honest-to-goodness ranch before."

"Oh, isn't she sweet!" cried Mollie fervently, adding, as one to whom inspiration had come: "I tell you what, Betty, we'll take her with us!"

"How sweet of you," drawled Grace. "Especially since the ranch belongs to her!"

The other girls chuckled and Mollie looked rather sheepish.

"Oh, well," she admitted, "I guess it would be a case of her taking us along."

"And I don't envy her the job," said gentle Amy unexpectedly, while the girls gazed their reproach.

"Betty," said Mollie, "there is one very important thing that I would like to know."

"Well, I'm the original little information bureau," Betty assured her. "What will you have?"

"Does your dad really want to sell the ranch? Or is your mother likely to win out?"

"Oh, mother always gets her way," said Betty confidently, adding: "Besides, the ranch was left to mother, you know, and not to dad. So really she has the say about it."

"Yes, but she might change her mind," said Grace pessimistically. "Fifteen thousand dollars is a lot of money, you know. She might decide to sell the ranch, after all."

"Well," said Betty, with an air of importance that the girls were quick to notice, "there is another reason why mother will probably hold on to the property, for a little while at least."

"Yes?" they queried eagerly.

"You see," Betty continued thoughtfully, "mother has an idea that this John Josephs is a little too anxious to buy the ranch. It's right up in the gold region, you know——"

"Gold!" shrieked Mollie. "You never said a word about gold, Betty Nelson! Do you mean there may be gold——"

"Now she *is* getting interesting," admitted Grace, shaken out of her usual calm.

"How romantic," murmured Amy, breathing fast.

"Yes," said Betty ruefully. "That's what dad says mother is—romantic! He says there isn't a chance in a thousand that there is real gold anywhere near that ranch——"

"Stop, woman, stop!" cried Mollie, with her most tragic scowl. "Wouldst put an end to all our dreams in one fell swoop——"

"Probably that is all we shall do—just dream," said Betty, insisting upon being practical. "It's an idea of mother's, that's all. But she is really determined to see the ranch, at least, before she makes up her mind whether to sell or not. In fact," she hesitated, colored a little, then went on bravely, "dad has decided to send Allen out there to look up the title. There is some trouble about that, I think——"

"Oh, now we know why she is so anxious to be a little cow girl," teased Grace, while the others regarded Betty's pretty color gleefully.

"Oh, Betty, Betty!" cried Mollie, shaking her head dolefully, "you are altogether hopeless!"

For Allen Washburn, of whom Betty had spoken in connection with the ranch, was a very promising young lawyer. Also this promising young lawyer was very fond of Betty Nelson. And while the girls are shaking their heads over this fact a little time will be taken to describe the Outdoor Girls to those readers who have not already met them and to review briefly the many and varied adventures they had had up to this time.

Betty Nelson, dark-haired, dark-eyed, and rosy-cheeked, was the natural leader of the four Outdoor Girls, a fact which had led to her being dubbed "Little Captain" by the adoring girls. Betty's father, Charles Nelson, had made a good deal of money in his manufacture of carpets, and Betty's mother was a very sweet lady whom the name of Rose fitted exactly.

Next came Mollie Billette, dark-haired and with snapping black eyes, who was almost as French in her manner as her very French mother.

Readers of the present volume must already feel very well acquainted with Grace Ford. Grace was the Gibson type, tall and slender and fair-haired and very pretty, with a decided liking for looking in mirrors.

Last of the quartette came Amy Blackford. Amy was the ward of John and Sarah Stonington, and for a long time she had thought her own name was Stonington. The mystery of her past had been cleared up, however, and Amy had come into her own. Shy, gentle, sweet, she was beloved and protected by the more hardy and active Betty and Mollie. And Amy, as shy girls sometimes will, had begun to think very much of Grace Ford's attractive brother, Will—which is a reminder that it is time to introduce "the boys."

Allen Washburn and his open fondness for Betty have already been spoken of. Allen was tall, nearly six feet. Sunburned and handsome of face and quick of action, Allen attracted every one wherever he went. And, truly, Betty was no exception to this rule! Allen had been one of the first to volunteer his services to the good old army of the U. S. A., and while he had gone over only a buck private, he had come back a lieutenant.

There was Will Ford, Grace's brother, whom Grace and Amy both adored. Will had been in the secret service when our country entered the war, and because of this he had been the victim of considerable misunderstanding. Afterward he had joined the army with the other boys. This was after some skillful secret service work that won the praise of the government, as well as the fervent admiration of the boys and girls.

The other two boys were Frank Haley and Roy Anderson who had come into the little group because of their friendship for Will and Allen. They were fine, clean-cut, likable boys, who had come through the war with colors flying.

The young folks had lived all their lives in Deepdale, a thriving little city with a population of about fifteen thousand people and situated in the heart of New York State. Deepdale was situated on the Argono River, a beautiful and romantic stream where pleasure craft of all sorts disported themselves. A branch line of the railroad connected with the main line directly to what the four Outdoor Girls believed to be the most wonderful of all cities, New York.

The name of "Outdoor Girls" had come to the quartette from the fact that they invariably spent their summer vacations, and winter holidays also, in some sort of outdoor sport. They could ride, swim, play tennis, drive, and, in fact, do everything that is expected of the athletic young girl of to-day.

They would never forget that first tramping tour when they had tramped for miles over the country, meeting with a great many unusual adventures on the way, as related in the first volume of this series, entitled, "The Outdoor Girls of Deepdale." Nor those other times at Rainbow Lake, in Florida, at Ocean View, and later at Pine Island, where they had come across that marvelous, mysterious gypsy cave.

Then had come the war with the boys on the other side, and the girls doing their "bit" at a Hostess House. And a little later what black distress overwhelmed them, when Will Ford was reported wounded and Allen's name was among the missing! This all happened while they were at Bluff Point taking a much-needed vacation from their work at the Hostess House.

In the volume directly preceding this, entitled "The Outdoor Girls at Wild Rose Lodge," the girls had had same very exciting experiences. An old man, Professor Dempsey, by name, who had retired to a little log cabin in the woods to recover his health, had chanced to do the girls a very great favor. Of course the girls were grateful to him and were very much interested when he told them of his two sons who were in the war. Later, when the girls read of the death of his two sons in the paper, they went to the old man's lonely cabin in the woods, but found themselves too late. According to a friendly neighbor, the old man had become temporarily insane at the terrible news, had wrecked his cabin in an insane frenzy, and disappeared.

Later, at Wild Rose Lodge, the girls were frightened several times by a strange apparition lurking in the woods around the lodge and Moonlight Falls, a beautiful fall of water not far from the cottage where the girls were staying. Later the boys came home from France and helped the girls solve the mystery.

And now here was Betty proposing another outing that promised to be more fun than any the Outdoor Girls had had yet. No wonder that in the clamor of their excited questions and answers no one heard the telephone ringing noisily in the hall.

Finally the Nelsons' maid came trudging up the stairs to answer it herself.

"If I can hear myself think," she grumbled, as she took the receiver from the hook. "With all them girls a-gabberin' an' a-talkin' at the top o' their lungs. Hello—I can't hear you—you'll have to talk louder—you don't know the noise they is in this house. Miss Betty?—jus' a minute——"

"A gen'leman to speak to you, Miss Betty," she announced a moment later, looking in on the hilarious girls. "An' le's hope you can hear him better'n I could, that's all," she grumbled, as Betty pushed by her in the doorway and gave her a friendly pat on the shoulder.

"Oh, they'll keep quiet now, all right," she said, with a laughing glance over her shoulder at her chums. "They'll want to hear what I have to say."

At which taunt the girls started such a dreadful clamor that she really had all she could do to hear Allen at the other end of the wire. Oh, yes, it was Allen!

"Sech a noise," grumbled the maid, as she trudged down the steps again. "I never did see sech wild uns!"

"Hello, hello, Allen," called Betty into the telephone. "The girls are here and—what's that? At Walnut Street? All right, that will be fine. I can't talk now. Tell you why later. Yes, we'll be there. Don't be silly. Good-by!"

Her face was flushed when she confronted the girls again.

"The boys have a half holiday—it's Saturday, you know," she told them, while they regarded her mischievously. "And they want us to pick them up in the car, get some lunch somewhere, and make a day of it. I told him we would."

"By 'him' I suppose you mean Allen," said Mollie, to which Betty ducked her a bow and the other girls giggled. "I like their nerve wanting us to pick them up. Why doesn't Frank come for us in his big car?"

"Allen figured it would take too long for them to come home and get it."

"My, they must be in a hurry to see us," said Grace, with a simper that sent the girls off into gales of laughter.

"Well," said Betty finally, "are you coming, or are you not?"

For answer Mollie jumped up, pressed a hat upon Grace's indignant head, handed Amy her coat, and crushed her own sport hat down on her dark hair.

"Be this our answer," she said dramatically.

CHAPTER III

ENTER PETER LEVINE

It is to be feared that the boys did not have as pleasant a time on that Saturday afternoon motor drive as they had hoped to have. For, whereas the girls should have showered their attentions upon them, the boys, they insisted upon talking about nothing but Gold Run Ranch, which was the name of the property left to Mrs. Nelson by her great uncle.

"You aren't very complimentary to us," Frank grumbled, as he hunched himself over the wheel of Mollie's car. "You seem mighty glad to go out to this forsaken old ranch where you won't see us for the whole summer."

"I guess we can stand it if you can," Mollie responded lightly, which only caused him to glower the more.

"Now I'll say Allen knew what he was doing when he studied law," remarked Roy Anderson gloomily, as he glanced over his shoulder at young Allen Washburn, who was driving Betty's neat little roadster with Betty herself beside him. "He sure falls in soft on this job."

"Meaning, I suppose," drawled Grace, "that he will have the pleasure of our company at Gold Run Ranch. Never mind, old boy, you needn't look so dreadfully gloomy. Have a chocolate and brace up."

"You give it to me," said Roy, laughing. Grace obediently popped a large juicy one into his mouth. It may be remarked that after this performance he really did look more cheerful.

"Anyway, we'll be back sometime, I suppose," said Mollie, continuing on the subject that was uppermost in her mind.

"Yes, if we don't run away with some of those handsome cowboys," put in Amy, with a chuckle. "Betty says they abound around Gold Run Ranch."

The girls giggled, but Will looked fierce.

"You had better not," he said, and though his look was for all the girls, Amy knew that the words were for her. She colored prettily and promised with her eyes that she wouldn't.

Grace caught this by-play as she munched a chocolate grumpily. Adoring her brother Will as she did, she had always been a little jealous of his fancy for Amy.

"Anyway, they don't have to be so silly in public," she told herself resentfully. As she roused herself from her musing, she heard Mollie say, with a laugh:

"Don't be surprised if we come home with our pockets full of gold. Mrs. Nelson thinks there is some of it about there."

"Oh, are you still talking about that silly old ranch?" Grace broke in petulantly. "I don't know why you are getting so excited about it when there is more than a chance that we sha'n't go at all."

"Hooray!" cried Frank, and stepped on the accelerator.

Mollie, beside him, turned to look at him coldly.

"I'm glad you feel that way about it, Frank Haley," she said primly. "But I'm very sorry to say we don't."

"Now, I have put my foot in it," cried Frank ruefully, turning his irresistible smile full upon her. "What shall I do to make up, Mollie? Hold your hand or something?"

His free hand closed over hers, but she snatched her own away with indignation that ended in a chuckle.

"Tend to your knitting," she warned him. "Didn't you see that we almost ran over that dog?"

But however much they might joke about the possibility of their not realizing their dreams for the summer, the Outdoor Girls were really worried about it, and the next few days were anxious ones for them.

Suppose Mrs. Nelson should yield to her husband's arguments and resolve to sell the ranch after all? For awhile it almost seemed as though she were about to do this very thing, and the suspense nearly drove the girls frantic.

Then something happened to turn the tide in their direction. And how the girls afterwards blessed that loud-necktied, check-suited man!

It was Betty who came to the door to admit this angel in disguise, it being the hired girl's day out. Her first glance at the stranger served to stamp him as one of those loud-voiced, flashily dressed persons commonly referred to as "sports," and at this first glance Betty took a violent dislike to him.

However, being accustomed to treat every one with kindliness, she asked him gravely whom he wished to see.

"Is Mrs. Nelson at home?" he asked ingratiatingly.

"Why, yes," hesitated Betty, then her natural courtesy getting the better of the dislike she felt for this person, she added politely: "Won't you come in? I will call mother."

With blandly murmured thanks the owner of the checked suit stepped over the threshold, his eyes still on Betty to such an extent that she was glad to be able to slip upstairs out of his sight.

"Mother," she explained hurriedly, finding that lady in her pretty dressing room, "there's a horrid person downstairs who wants to see you. I don't like his looks, and if you don't want to see him I can tell him you aren't at home——"

"Heavens, Betty, is he as bad as all that?" asked Mrs. Nelson, as she rose hastily and gave an automatic pat to her hair. "I hope he doesn't steal the silver. You shouldn't have left him alone, dear——

" and with these words she swept out of the room and down the stairs.

Betty heard her greet the man, and then slipped off to her own room and picked up some half-finished embroidery.

"I hope he doesn't bother mother too much," she mused aloud. "I never saw a more unpleasant looking person in my life. I wonder what he can want, anyway."

It was fully half an hour later that she heard the closing door downstairs that told her their unwelcome visitor had left. A minute later her mother herself opened the door of Betty's room, looking so troubled and unsettled that Betty jumped to her feet in quick alarm.

"Mother, did that man say anything to make you feel bad?" she cried. "Because, if he did——"

"No, no, dear," said Mrs. Nelson, sinking into a chair, while her eyes sought the window thoughtfully. "I am worried, that's all."

Betty drew a low chair over beside her mother, and, sitting down, took Mrs. Nelson's hand in both her own.

"Tell me, dear," she urged.

Mrs. Nelson drew her troubled gaze away from the window and looked at the Little Captain intently.

"Betty," she said, "there is something strange about this Gold Run Ranch of ours. This man——"

"Yes?" prompted Betty, as her mother paused.

"This man who called this morning wanted to buy the ranch for a western client of his. It seems this client is willing to pay me my own price—within reasonable limits of course. He seemed so strangely eager to make a deal with me——"

"Yes?" prompted Betty again, beginning to look worried herself.

"Well," continued Mrs. Nelson, "I decided then and there that I wouldn't sell to anybody."

"Oh, Mother!" Betty was all eagerness now, "do you really mean it?"

"Yes, I do," said Mrs. Nelson, determination replacing uncertainty. "There must be something unusual about Gold Run or John Josephs and this man, too, wouldn't be so anxious to get it away from me. I am certainly not going to let them drive me into selling, until I see my property at least."

"Good for you, Mother!" cried Betty enthusiastically. "I've been fearfully worried for fear you wouldn't see it that way. Did you tell the man in the check suit that?"

"No, I didn't," said Mrs. Nelson, smiling as she pressed Betty's hand. "Now you will see what a schemer your mother is, my dear. I told him I hadn't definitely decided yet on any course, that I had already had a very good offer for my ranch, and that he would have to see Allen Washburn, our attorney. I wanted Allen to have a chance to size this man up and see if he has the same impression of him that I had."

"Mother," breathed Betty admiringly, "I think you are wonderful." Then after a little pause, she added shyly: "You really think a great deal of—of Allen's ability, don't you, Mother?"

"I do, dear," said Mrs. Nelson, stroking the brown head gently. Then she added with a hint of mischief in her voice: "Your father and I have come to feel toward him almost as if he were our son."

"Oh—" murmured Betty, very faintly.

Two days went by—anxious ones for the girls. In the Nelson home, this time in the pretty living room, Allen Washburn was now a guest.

"Well," Mrs. Nelson said, with more than a hint of eagerness in her voice, "what did you think of our loudly-dressed friend, Allen?"

"Was he as bad as Mrs. Nelson's description makes him out to be?" asked Mr. Nelson, smiling genially through a cloud of cigar smoke.

Betty, in a corner of the lounge, was trying her best to be calm while she waited eagerly for Allen's reply.

"I don't know just how Mrs. Nelson described this fellow to you, I'm sure," he answered, with a smiling glance toward Betty's mother. "But I'm quite sure that she didn't say anything bad enough."

"Then you didn't like him either?" asked Mrs. Nelson quickly.

"I neither liked him nor trusted him," Allen replied decidedly, adding with a wry smile: "He calls himself Peter Levine, but I'm willing to wager about anything I have that that isn't his real name."

"You think he's a sharper then?" Mr. Nelson interjected.

"Yes, sir," responded Allen, his young face earnestly intent. "He looks to me like one of these confidence men who abound in the western boom towns—men who can talk the other fellow into putting his last cent into some 'sure thing.' 'Sure thing,'" he repeated disgustedly. "The only sure thing about most of those schemes is the certainty of 'going bust' and losing every penny you have in the world."

"And yet," Mr. Nelson commented, "these sharpers, 'confidence men,' as you call them, often manage to keep just within the law."

"Oh yes," said Allen, "they manage to keep the letter of the law—sometimes. But that is just a caution to save their own necks. It's the spirit of the law that they violate. But we are getting away from the point," he added, pulling himself up short with an apologetic smile toward Mrs. Nelson. "We were speaking of this Peter Levine. My summing up of him is that he is entirely untrustworthy."

Mrs. Nelson shot a triumphant glance at her husband.

"You see?" she said. "I was sure Allen would agree with me."

"Of course I may be mistaken," Allen continued, rather hesitantly. "But I have a very distinct impression, a sort of seventh sense we fellows in the law game call it, that this Levine is in league with John Josephs, the man that offered you fifteen thousand for the ranch."

"Oh!" said Mrs. Nelson, startled. "How can you know that?"

"I don't know it," Allen told her. "I only suspect."

"Then what would you advise us to do?"

"Hold tight and not sell till you have had a chance to look matters over on the ground—not from a distance."

"Well," said Mr. Nelson rising resignedly and knocking the ashes from his cigar, "I suppose that settles it. I shall have to leave my business to go to smash," he added, with a chuckle, "while I take my family into a barbarous land where every second man you meet has designs on a well-filled pocketbook——"

But he got no further, for Betty had run over to him and turned him imperiously around till his smiling eyes looked down into her gleeful ones.

"Daddy," she cried, "do you really mean it? We can all go to Gold Run—you and mother and the girls? We'll have to have the girls, you know!" she ended on a pleading note.

"Oh yes, of course," said Mr. Nelson resignedly. "We will have to have the girls."

It was a very radiant Betty who, a few minutes later, saw Allen Washburn to the door.

"And to think," she murmured, while Allen smiled down at her, "that I didn't like that perfect angel, Peter Levine, at first. Why, I should have welcomed him with open arms!"

"Why?" asked Allen, taken by surprise.

"Don't you know?" asked Betty, mischievously wide-eyed. "If he hadn't happened along just when he did our glorious adventure would have dwindled into a might-have-been. Why, I could love him for it."

"Good-night, I'm going!" ejaculated Allen, and before Betty could gasp he had flung out of the door.

"Where are you going?" she called, laughter in her voice.

"To kill Peter Levine," growled a voice out of the darkness, and Betty, closing the door very softly, chuckled to herself.

CHAPTER IV

AN IMITATION HOLD-UP

It was all over. The bustling days of preparation for the long trip, during which the girls had hardly had time to give vent to their excitement, had passed, and here they were actually finding their places in the puffing, western bound train.

"Here's number five," Grace said, as she slid into a velvet-covered seat with a sigh of thankfulness. "Who is coming in here with me?"

"Guess I'm elected," laughed Betty. "And here's number seven for Mollie and Amy, and mother and dad are in six right across the way. That completes the family party."

They were hardly settled when there was a last warning cry of "All aboard" and the train began to move ever so slowly from the station.

The girls peered out to wave good-by to the boys and some of their other friends who had come to see them off. The young fellows looked rather gloomy—all except Allen. The latter shouted something that they took to be "See you later!" and then the train swept around a curve, hiding the station from view.

"Well," said Grace, with a sigh, as she opened her grip to fish for the inevitable candy box, "the boys seemed to take our flitting pretty hard. They looked as if we were already dead and buried."

"Far from it," murmured Betty happily, her eyes on the ever changing view from the window. "I feel as if we were just beginning to live."

The hours of the morning passed like minutes to the girls, and they were surprised when the porter came through with his "Foist call fo' dinnah!"

The afternoon passed uneventfully, and they amused themselves by making up stories about their fellow passengers. There was the quaint little man in number four who reminded them of Professor Arnold Dempsey and who might very easily have been a professor, judging from the number of books he carried.

Then there was the freckled-faced small boy in number three whose antics kept his mother in a continual state of "nerves." Once when he bounced one of those implements commonly known as "spit balls" off of the bookish little man's bald head, the girls thought they would die trying to stifle their merriment.

Then there was the very pretty, but much be-powdered and rouged girl behind them in number nine. Grace embarrassed Betty very much by turning around to look at her every five minutes or so.

"She's a moving picture actress or something, I'm sure of it," Grace confided in Betty's unsympathetic ear. "I wonder if I could fix my hair the way she does. She fascinates me."

"She seems to," Betty retorted dryly, adding with a twinkle. "You may be able to fix your hair like hers—though I doubt it—but please remember that your mother doesn't want you to use rouge."

"Well, you know I wouldn't do that," said Grace in a huff, adding maliciously, "I guess you are just jealous, that's all."

"Uh-huh, that must be it," said Betty, with an unruffled good-nature that made Grace secretly ashamed of herself.

"I'm sorry, Betty," she said after a rather long pause, adding generously: "You don't need to be jealous of anybody."

"Thanks," Betty answered, with a smile. "I knew you didn't mean it, dear."

And so the long hours of the afternoon wore away, dusk came, shrouding the swiftly moving landscape in a veil of mystery. So engrossed were the girls in contemplation of the changing beauty of nature that it seemed almost sacrilege when the blatant lights of the train flashed forth, bringing them violently back to a realization of time and place.

"Don't you want any supper?" Mr. Nelson was asking, in his pleasant voice. "It isn't like the Outdoor Girls to overlook meal time."

"Far be it from us to spoil our good reputation," cried Mollie buoyantly, and away they rushed to the dressing room to wash for supper. Though dining on a train was no novelty to the girls, they never lost the keenness of their first delight in the experience.

"It's fascinating," Mollie remarked once, spearing desperately at an elusive potato as the train jerked and jolted over the rails at sixty miles an hour, "to see how often you can raise your coffee cup without spilling the coffee all over your food!"

On this night at supper Mollie was so screamingly funny that the girls had all they could do to keep their hilarity from making them conspicuous.

Mr. and Mrs. Nelson at a table for two across the aisle smiled indulgently at their charges, and once Mrs. Nelson met her husband's glance and chuckled fondly.

"Pretty nice set of girls?" she said softly.

"Pretty nice!" Mr. Nelson agreed.

"I'm beginning to wish we were at Gold Run now," confided Mollie, after dining. She and Amy had slipped into the seat opposite Betty and Grace.

"Oh, I think it's all fun," cried Betty, for she was always the last of the Outdoor Girls to feel tired. "We change at Chicago to-morrow afternoon," she added. "And then two more nights on the train, and then Gold Run!"

"Oh, that sounds good," cried Mollie, adding eagerly: "Tell me, Betty, shall we be able to choose any horse we want for our own particular mount?"

"Oh, yes," said Betty, adding with a smile: "It will be interesting to see the kind of horse each one of you will choose. Amy will like the gentle one, Grace will choose hers for its looks and yours will be the most vicious one in the pack, Mollie."

"Well, I like that!" said Mollie unperturbed. "She wants to kill me off even before I get there."

"Pack?" murmured Amy. "Is a 'pack' of horses right?" But no one answered her.

"I wonder," mused Grace dreamily, "if there will be a tan one—all tan, you know, without even a spot of any other color——"

"Oh, of course," laughed Betty. "If we haven't an all tan one in the corrals at Gold Run, we'll send to the nearest ranch and have one imported for you. Don't worry your little head about that."

A little while after that they stopped at a water station, and most of the passengers got off to stretch their cramped limbs. And, as the conductor informed them that they would be there for fifteen minutes at least, the girls followed the general example.

However, in their enthusiasm at finding the good old solid earth under their feet once more, they wandered too far, and the warning toot of the starting train found them quite a distance from the platform.

They had not earned the title of Outdoor Girls for nothing, however, and by sprinting for all they were worth they were able to make the last car just in the nick of time.

"Whew, that was a close call," said Betty as they made their way, panting, through to their own car, where Mr. and Mrs. Nelson were looking frantically for them. "No more water stations for us."

Darkness fell, and the porters moved about, making up berths and answering the hundred and one insistent calls of the passengers. [

The girls went to bed with no protest whatever and were soon sleeping the sleep of healthy youth. It was toward midnight that they were rather rudely jerked out of this beautiful sleep by a sudden and almost violent stopping of the train.

Betty, who was sleeping in a lower berth, she and Grace having decided to take turns, sat up and peered out of the grimed window into the gloom. No station lights greeted her, as she expected confidently they would. Nothing but inky, startling blackness.

That she was not the only one roused was proved by the subdued sound of voices raised in sleepy protest.

"They ought to put that engineer in prison for stopping like that," said a man's voice.

"Gee! I thought it was a wreck, sure," came another surly voice.

At this moment a couple of legs dangled themselves over the side of Betty's berth and in another minute the owner of them slid down beside Betty. Betty giggled nervously, but Grace clutched her arm and shook it.

"Listen!" she said. "There's nothing to laugh about. This is a hold-up, that's what it is! You know what your father said about there being a lot of them around this place."

That this conclusion had been reached by some one else in the car was proved by a woman's voice that rose shrilly above the rest.

"It's a hold-up, that's what it is!" she cried, adding, with what seemed to Betty ridiculous panic: "Oh, what shall I do, what shall I do?"

"Better stop making a fuss, first off," growled another masculine voice, and again Betty giggled nervously.

"Goodness, I hope I don't have to get out in my nightie," she said, and poked her head out through the curtains.

"Look out," warned Grace, pulling her back. "You may get shot or something."

"Don't be silly," retorted Betty, not altogether decided whether to be frightened or amused by the situation. "There isn't anything out there but a lot of funny looking heads sticking through the curtains."

"I don't see how you can laugh about it," said Grace, through chattering teeth. "I don't think it would be any j-joke to have all our m-money taken from us——"

"Sh-h—be quiet," warned Betty, peeping again through the slit in the curtain. "Somebody's coming. Listen!"

Grace listened, and so, evidently, did every one else in the car. No wonder that, scared though she undoubtedly was, Betty found humor in the situation. Heads of every kind and description stuck through the curtains, women's, some in boudoir caps, some without, men's heads, either bald or with hair grotesquely ruffled by sleep, and on every face depicted every one of the varied emotions which have disturbed the human race since time began.

And there they were, all frozen to immobility by the sound of two men's voices raised in heated discussion.

Then the owners of the voices came into view, and the expression on all the faces changed to bewildered amazement. Instead of the masked bandit which they had half expected to see there was a very portly and very excited gentleman and with him was a conductor, not so portly but just as excited.

"I tell you," the conductor was saying, his face red with wrath, "you are violating the rules of the company by flagging this train for a personal matter——"

"You have told me that before," roared the portly gentleman, waxing almost apoplectic. "And I've told you I don't care a hang for the rules of the company. What I want to find is my daughter and that young scamp she ran away with. And if you don't help me, I'll wring your neck!"

"I tell you there is no couple answering your description on this train," rasped the conductor, as the two made their way, shouting and gesticulating, through the two rows of amazed heads and so on into the next car.

"Well, I'll be blowed," commented the voice belonging to one of the heads; and as if that were a signal, all the other heads promptly withdrew to the accompaniment of exclamations and laughter.

In the darkness of the berth Betty chuckled.

"Oh, they did look so funny, Gracie," she said. "All those people with their heads stuck out into the aisle. You should have taken a peek."

"Humph," grunted Grace, unsympathetically, as she prepared to climb into her berth again. Then she said: "I hope if that man's daughter takes a notion to run away again, she won't do it on our train, that's all!"

CHAPTER V

THE HANDSOME COWBOY

Next morning the girls were hilarious over the mirthful episode in the train the night before. Betty and Mollie "took off" the expressions on the faces of their fellow passengers till Amy and Grace shouted with glee.

"Oh, stop it, you two," gasped Grace, finally. "I'm sore from laughing. I think you would make a hit as clowns in a circus."

"My, isn't she complimentary?" lisped Mollie, and the girls went off in fresh gales of merriment.

"I wish," said Grace, after a pause, "that we were going to reach Gold Run this afternoon, instead of Chicago. I'm half afraid to spend another night in the sleeper after the scare we got last night. It might be a *real* bandit this time."

"Oh, what would we care?" said Betty carelessly. "I'd rather like to meet a train robber, myself."

"About all a bandit could do would be to take our money," added Mollie.

"All!" cried Grace indignantly. "Yes, that's all. And what would we do without any money, I'd like to know!"

"Goodness, we could always sell the ranch," said Betty, so matter-of-factly that the girls chuckled. "We have Peter Levine to fall back on, you know."

"'Peter Levine,'" repeated Amy, then added quickly: "Oh yes, he was the man who wanted your mother to sell the ranch."

"Yes, and it was too bad of you to keep him all to yourself, Betty," said Grace reproachfully.

"You might at least have shown him to the rest of us."

"He wasn't anything to show," said Betty, experiencing again the feeling of distaste she had had for the man. "He was one of the most unpleasant looking men I ever saw. Just the same," she added lightly, "we owe him a lot. If it hadn't been for him we probably wouldn't be sitting in this beautiful train, speeding to our great adventure. I told Allen I could almost love Peter Levine for it."

"You did?" queried Mollie, her eyes dancing. "What did he say?"

"He left me rather suddenly," said Betty, with a chuckle at the memory. "He said he was on his way to kill Peter."

"Poor Allen," laughed Grace. "It must be awful to be that way. When is he coming out to Gold Run, Betty?"

"As soon as he finishes this case he is on now," answered Betty, flushing in spite of herself as she thought of Allen. "There is really no great hurry about it, you know. Dad has made up his mind to take a regular vacation while he's about it, and I imagine mother won't care if she never gets home."

That afternoon they changed trains at Chicago, bemoaning the fact that they had not time to see something of the great city before they traveled farther west. There was only half an hour between trains and, as every one knows, there can be little sightseeing done in that limited space of time. As it was, for some reason they could not ascertain, the outgoing train was over an hour late in starting. If they had known this fact in advance they might have managed to spend their time more profitably than in cooling their heels in the station waiting room.

As it was, it was a rather disgruntled set of girls who boarded the train for Gold Run and allowed Mr. Nelson and the porter to find their seats for them.

"I don't see why trains can't be on time," grumbled Mollie, as she peered at the rather distorted image of herself in the narrow mirror between the windows. "Here it is nearly seven o'clock and I'm as hungry as a bear."

"Well," said Betty, cheerfully, "something tells me they have a diner on this train. Come on, girls, let's wash our hands and get something to eat."

The girls hardly knew which they enjoyed the most, their dinner or the novel scenery that slipped past them so swiftly. It was their first venture into this part of the world, and they found the initiation fascinating.

"The trouble is," complained Amy, "it will be dark before long and we'll have to miss all this," with an expressive sweep of her hand toward the car window.

"It is too bad," said Betty, regretfully adding, with a light laugh: "If we were only like the princess in the story, the members of whose royal house never slept, we would probably see more of the scenery."

That night the girls proved that Grace was not alone in her fondness for sleep. There being no more interruptions in the shape of fuming gentlemen on the trail of runaway daughters, they slept soundly through the long hours while the train plunged onward through the inky blackness of the night. They did not stir until the sun, shining on their faces, roused them to the realization that another beautiful day had dawned.

That is, it was beautiful up to noon. Then it clouded down, and they ate lunch while the rain dashed furiously on the windows of the dining car.

"I am thankful we are under cover," said Betty.

"Fancy riding on the ranch in this rain," put in Amy.

"No life in the saddle for me when it rains," broke in Grace.

During the afternoon the girls napped and read. When the time came to get supper they were glad to see that they had run away from the storm and the sun was setting clearly.

"Funny, how sleepy one gets," drawled Grace, about nine o'clock. "I'll not stay up late."

No one wanted to do that, and in less than an hour all were sleeping soundly while the long train rumbled along on its trip westward.

"And this is the day," breathed Mollie the next noon, as they made their way from the dining car through some half dozen other cars to their own. "Betty, I feel as if I couldn't wait to see your beautiful ranch."

"I wonder," said Grace as they dropped into their seats once more, "if those cowboys are really as good-looking as you say, Betty. I must admit," she added, as she viewed the rather monotonous landscape petulantly, "I haven't seen anything that looks like a cowboy yet."

"Goodness, hear the child!" cried Betty airily. "She hasn't been near a ranch, yet she expects to see whole droves of cow-punchers——"

"Look," Mollie interrupted, grasping her arm. They were slowing down at a station and there were no less than three picturesque looking young fellows loitering about the place. One was astride an extremely nervous horse that shied as the train puffed to a standstill and rose on his hind legs as though trying his best to shake his rider off. "There's a real show for you," Mollie cried joyfully. "How does that look to you, Gracie? True to life?"

"Um, that's better," admitted Grace, while the girls craned their necks for a better view of the horseman. "Now if they only have that sort of thing at Gold Run——"

"Well, we'll have a chance to find out pretty soon whether they do or not," broke in Betty, the thrill of suppressed excitement in her voice. "Dad says we ought to get there in an hour."

"An hour!" wailed Amy, as the train jolted on its way once more and the romantic group on the station were lost to view. "And I thought we were almost there!"

But the hour passed more quickly than the girls had anticipated, for the view from the car windows, becoming more and more interesting, absorbed their attention. As a general rule the country was flat, but now and then in the background could be caught glimpses of heavily wooded mountain ranges that would offer chances for all sorts of adventures to the four eager Outdoor Girls.

"I wonder if there are wild animals in those woods," said Amy, her eyes widening at the thought. "Real ones."

"You don't suppose they import stuffed ones, do you?" asked Grace dryly.

"Of course there are wild animals—lots of 'em," said Betty, feeling more and more gloriously excited as they neared their destination. "Maybe we can borrow a gun or two from the cow-punchers and have a shot at 'em—animals, I mean, not cow-punchers," she explained, with a giggle.

On top of these rather wild imaginings came Mr. Nelson, telling them it was time to get their things together, for they were within a few minutes of Gold Run.

"I know how long it takes you girls to put a hat on," he laughed. "So I think you had better start right away."

Then—Gold Run! with the dash for the door and Grace running back to rescue a half-empty but still precious candy box and

Mollie wanting to know if Amy would please stop pressing her suitcase in the middle of her back——

Someway, Mr. Nelson managed to get them all safely to the station platform, whereupon he breathed a sigh of relief.

"Whew! that's the hardest job you ever gave me, Rose," he remarked to his wife, with a chuckle.

Here, as at most of the other stations, was a handful of cowboys who had come to meet the train. One of these, a handsome young fellow, detached himself from the rest and approached Mrs. Nelson, sweeping off his sombrero as he did so.

"Mrs. Nelson, ma'am?" he asked in a soft drawl that captivated the girls immediately.

Mrs. Nelson smiled assent and the young fellow indicated a buckboard drawn up to the station.

"I brought the wagon," he said, with a grin that showed a beautiful set of white teeth. "An' some saddle hosses, thinkin' you might like to ride——"

However, the ladies decided on the buckboard, which was driven by a shy-eyed, sandy-haired young fellow who gave the girls one frightened glance and looked swiftly away again, for all the world, Mollie said afterwards, as if he expected them to bite him.

Mr. Nelson elected to ride horseback with Andy Rawlinson, which was the name of the good-looking cowboy.

As the driver chirruped to the horses and they clattered over the bumpy road, Grace turned to Betty with a smile.

"I have realized the ambition of a life time!" she said dramatically. "I have seen one handsome cowboy!"

CHAPTER VI

AT THE RANCH

To the girls, that jolting ride was like an adventure straight from the Arabian Nights. The fact that they were squeezed four in a seat which was meant to accommodate only three, served to dampen their enthusiasm not a trifle. Mrs. Nelson, riding in front with the bashful driver, vainly sought to engage him in conversation. After repeated failures she settled down to enjoy the ride in silence.

A dozen yards or so ahead of them Andy Rawlinson and Mr. Nelson cantered up the dusty road, their horses' hoofs making the dust fly in a white cloud.

"Goodness!" sneezed Betty, extracting a small handkerchief from her pocket and applying it to her nose, "I do hope those two keep their distance. We'll be simply choked with dust."

"I wonder," said Grace, as she rubbed her dust-filled eyes, "if they don't have any rain in this part of the world."

"Of course they do; only this happens to be the dry season," said Mollie, instructively, from the heights of her superior intelligence. At least, that is what she called it.

"I'll say it's dry," grumbled Grace.

"Ooh, look," Amy interrupted ecstatically. "Isn't that a cactus over there? Oh, I've wanted all my life to see some real cacti. Now I know we're in the West."

The girls were silent for a moment, gazing out over the rolling plain—a plain studded with stunted trees and sickly-looking bushes with here and there a cactus plant for variety's sake—out to the hazy mountains beyond, serene, calm, majestic, jutting jaggedly into the dazzling blue of a cloudless sky.

"The mountains!" murmured Betty, half to herself. "How I love them. The plains are fascinating in a cruelly romantic way, but somehow the mountains make one think of hidden springs rushing swiftly into noisy foolish little brooks, of bird songs, and the smell of cool damp earth, of the crackling of dry twigs under one's feet, and the pungent woodsy smell of camp fires—but there," she broke off confusedly, as she realized the girls were regarding her with fond amusement. "I didn't mean to wax so poetic."

"It's all right, honey," said Mollie, giving her hand a warm little squeeze. "You rave right along. I know just how you feel, for I get that way myself sometimes."

"There is something mighty wonderful about the mountains," added Grace softly.

"Oh, I love them, too," broke in Amy, adding with such earnestness that the girls looked at her wonderingly. "They are everything that Betty has said. And yet when Betty spoke of the plains as being cruel I couldn't help wondering if the mountains weren't sometimes like that, too."

"What do you mean?" they queried, with quick interest.

"I was thinking," Amy continued slowly, "that the mountains might not seem so kind to one who was lost in them—without a gun perhaps. I have heard Will say that a person who had no knowledge of woodcraft would find it almost impossible to recover his path, once he had lost it. And," she added, with a shudder, her eyes fixed steadily on the distant mountain range, "there are wild animals in those forests."

"Of course there are," agreed Betty lightly, as she saw how serious the girls' faces had become. "Oodles of foxes and bears and raccoons and things. Why, how would you expect to get pretty furs when you wanted them if those things didn't exist? Cheer up, Amy dear. We're a long way from being lost in the woods without a gun!"

A minute later the girls lost interest in everything but the immediate present. For, in the distance, but distinctly visible, loomed a long low ranch house which the silent driver beside Mrs. Nelson deigned to admit was on Gold Run Ranch.

"You see it, girls?" cried the lady, turning a beaming face to the girls. "You know, I feel just like a little girl with a beautiful new toy."

"And we're awfully glad you've got the toy, Mrs. Nelson," said Grace, fervently.

"Look," cried Mollie suddenly. "Your father and that cowboy are turning off from the main road. That must be where the ranch begins. Oh, girls, oh, girls, I'm glad I came!"

A few minutes later their jolting buckboard turned in after the two horsemen, and since the new road proved to be nothing but two deep ruts worn in the grass and as the ponies attached to the buckboard showed considerable excitement at coming near home, the girls found themselves holding on to each other convulsively to keep from being thrown out on the stubbly grass at the side of the road.

"Whew, I'm glad that's over!" exclaimed Mollie, as the driver drew in the rearing horses and spoke to them soothingly. "Come on, girls," she added, making ready to jump out. "I'm going to remove myself from this buckboard before one of those horses decides to sit in my lap."

The girls laughed and followed her with alacrity.

"Oh," cried Betty, hugging Amy ecstatically, simply because she happened to be the nearest one to hug. "There are the horse corrals over there! And, oh, girls! look at the cows, dozens and dozens and dozens of 'em. Mother," she cried, turning wide-eyed to the latter, "do all those 'anymiles' really belong to you?"

"I presume they do, dear," said Mrs. Nelson, her own face flushed with excitement. "I can't quite take in the amazing truth of it yet."

They were standing beside the first of a long line of low buildings that seemed little more than glorified sheds and which the girls decided must be the "bunk houses" for the ranch hands.

And while they were wondering if it would be possible to slip over to the corrals for a closer look at the horses, Mr. Nelson sauntered up to them, with handsome Andy Rawlinson keeping diffidently a little in the rear.

"It's nearly supper time," he informed them smiling. "And Andy here," he indicated young Rawlinson, who grinned an acknowledgment, "says that everybody has supper sharp on the minute of six. So what do you say if we go up to the house and have a little refreshment?"

The girls were not altogether reluctant to obey, much as they desired a closer look at the bronchos, for they realized that they were pretty hungry.

The ranch house was one of those quaint old structures which had begun as a tiny, one-story frame cottage and had gradually been added to until now it seemed, Betty said, to "spread all over the landscape." It had porches and doors in the most unexpected places, but the whole house was painted such an immaculate white and the shutters were such a friendly green that the effect of the place was indescribably charming.

"If the house is as clean inside as it looks outside," whispered Grace to Betty as Andy Rawlinson led them up on to one of the many porches, "I'll never dare go in. I never felt so mussy and dirty in all my life."

"Never mind, we're all in the same boat," said Betty encouragingly, and then they stepped into one of the pleasantest rooms they had ever seen.

It was big and cool and airy, in spite of the fact that supper preparations were going on at one end of it. Rough picturesque looking chairs were scattered about, and over near the windows a long table was invitingly set for six. And oh, the delicious odor of cooking things that was wafted on the air!

At sight of them a stout but immaculately neat and rosy-faced woman left whatever she was doing with a frying pan on the stove and came over to them, wiping her hands on her apron, her face wreathed in smiles.

"Go long with you, Andy Rawlinson," she cried as the youth lingered rather awkwardly in the doorway. "There's no need for you to tell me who these folks are, for I already know them for the new master and his lady and the young ladies, bless their pretty sweet faces. Come right in, all of you, and Lizzie here," turning to a wholesome-looking, mouse-haired girl who had come in from the other room, "Lizzie will take you to see the rooms and you can have your pick. But don't be long," she cautioned, as they started to follow Lizzie and she turned back to her frying pan on the stove, "for supper is all ready and you must be nearly famished."

If the girls had been impressed by the quaintness of this quaint old house from the outside, they were even more delighted by its interior.

They passed down a rather dark and narrow hall at the end of which were three low steps leading to such a series of rooms as the girls had never seen before, each furnished neatly but plainly, the only touch of color being the gay cretonne curtains at the windows. The rooms all seemed to be connected by doors and to reach these doors one was obliged to go up two steps or down three or up one, as the case might be.

"Goodness," cried Betty, when Lizzie had led the way through three of these quaint little rooms and the open doors seemed to reveal several others, "I wonder if all these rooms were really occupied."

"Yes, miss," said Lizzie, halting and speaking unexpectedly. "They was a time when these rooms wuz all filled. Old Mr. Barcolm"—this being the name of Mrs. Nelson's great uncle—"had a many children and grandchildren an' seemed like he was sot on 'em all livin' with him. But they got to quarrelin' and all left th' old man an' he was so mad he cut 'em all out o' his will. At least," she finished, as though warned by the intent look of her listeners that she had said more than she had intended to, "that's what they says. But mebbe it ain't the truth, fer all I knows."

Then she led them on again through the maze of rooms while the girls thought amazedly of what she had told them. Finally she came to a stop in a room, larger than the rest, and turned her rather stolid gaze upon Mr. and Mrs. Nelson.

"Miz Cummins," she announced, dully—the girls were afterward to find out that Cummins was the name of the rosy-faced woman who had met them so cordially at the door and who seemed to be general housekeeper for the place—"Miz Cummins thought as how this would be a good room fer the mister and missus. They is some nice rooms back of these fer the young ladies. She sed, if you liked any of the other rooms better, to take your pick. They's fresh water in the pitchers," indicating a washstand with a bowl and two pitchers of gleaming water upon it, "an' if you want anythin' else, you wuz please to tell me." And with these words, uttered so precisely that it sounded like a rehearsed speech, which, in fact, it was, Lizzie disappeared, leaving the travelers to themselves.

"Come on, girls," cried Betty, pushing them before her into the next room. "Let's see what kind of rooms 'Miz Cummins' has picked out for us."

They were not at all unusual rooms, being both about the same size and nearly square and furnished about as simply as they could possibly be.

"If it weren't for the different colored cretonne at the windows," said Mollie, with a chuckle, "these rooms might be twins. You and Grace can have the lavender cretonne, Amy, and Betty and I will take the blue."

"Don't those beds look heavenly?" sighed Grace, as she pulled off her hat and threw herself upon the big, snowy-sheeted bed.

"Goodness!" cried Amy, in dismay. "She's flopped. Get her up, somebody, before she gets the bed so dirty I can't sleep in it to-night."

For answer Betty made a dash for Grace, pulled her to her feet, and pushed her over to the washstand.

"See that water, Grace Ford?" she cried sternly. "Now use it!"

"And make it snappy," added Mollie slangily, as she and Betty disappeared into the adjoining room. "I can smell 'Miz Cummins'" cooking clear in here!

CHAPTER VII

A SUDDEN STORM

The girls spent the rest of that day getting acquainted, at which agreeable task Andy Rawlinson, the head cowboy, assisted pleasantly. The latter introduced them to several others of the ranch hands, all of whom were as picturesque and good-natured as Andy himself.

Escorted by Rawlinson and followed by the admiring glances of the other cowboys, the girls were introduced to the interior of the bunk houses which, with their rude wooden cots built into the side of the walls, their scanty and rather severe furniture, and the romantic looking trophies fastened to the bare boards of the walls, filled the girls with curiosity and interest.

Then on to the corrals, where some spectacular broncho busting was staged for the sole benefit of the visitors. In this dangerous business Andy himself took a part, and the girls gasped with dismay and later with admiration as the boy ran alongside a vicious looking animal for a few paces, then flung himself recklessly upon the beast's back and clung there, seemingly defying all the laws of gravitation.

"Oh, he surely will be killed!" cried Amy, clutching Betty in terror. "That horse will throw him——"

"Keep quiet, can't you, Amy?" cried Mollie impatiently, beside herself with excitement. "Don't you suppose he has ever done this sort of thing before?"

Then followed such an exhibition of sheer grit and skill and dauntless courage as none of the girls would ever forget.

The vicious brute raced madly around and around the corrals, cruel head upflung, nostrils dilated, but still the man upon his back clung with maddening persistence. Then he stopped so suddenly that the man was almost flung over his lowered head and the girls held their breath, but Andy recovered himself and touching the spurs to the beast's belly, sent it flying round the corral once more. There was sweat on its body and the flaring nostrils were blood red with the effort, but the spirit of the beast was still unbroken.

Around and around the ring he plunged, the other horses galloping wildly from his path, then suddenly as though the thing on his back had maddened him past bearing, he began to buck and to plunge and to rear himself on his hind legs in a desperate effort to throw himself backward, until it seemed to the fascinated, terrified girls that Andy Rawlinson surely must be killed.

HE CLUNG TO THE HORSE'S BACK AS THOUGH HE HAD
BEEN A PART OF HIM.

The Outdoor Girls in the Saddle.

But Andy Rawlinson had not spent his twenty-eight years in the
saddle for nothing. He clung to that horse's back as though he had

been a part of him, and when the outraged beast tried to throw himself over backward for the second time, Andy evidently decided that he had played enough.

A cruel blow of his spurred heel brought the beast almost to its knees with a whinny of pain. Then it jumped high in the air, and once more began its furious race with this mysterious and horrible being that clung so tenaciously to his back.

Andy rode him hard, cruelly hard, and when the beast, panting, sweating, beaten, would have stopped he dug the spurs in and drove him on, on, until the broncho's breath came in sobbing gasps and his legs trembled under him.

Betty, who could never bear to see anything hurt, shouted to Andy Rawlinson as man and beast came abreast of her:

"Isn't that enough?" she cried. "You've beaten him. Stop! Please stop!"

And Andy Rawlinson, flashing his pleasant smile, flung himself from his mount, while the beautiful horse stood there, quivering, head hung in shame——

"Game hoss, that," said Andy, as he vaulted the low railing and approached the girls. "Fought like a thoroughbred."

"And you were wonderful," cried Betty, with her warm impulsiveness. "I never saw finer riding. We were all afraid you were going to be killed."

Andy was pleased, but he looked at Betty rather quizzically.

"Strange," he drawled, with a smile on his face, "strange what impressions you get sometimes. Now I kind o' thought you was mad at me, the way you called out to stop. Anyways, you looked mad."

"I was only sorry for the horse," Betty explained gravely. "He was game, as you say, and I hated to see his spirit entirely broken."

Andy Rawlinson looked at her with admiring approval in his nice eyes.

"There speaks the real lover of animals," he cried enthusiastically. "I hate to break a good hoss myself, but you see it has to be done— for the sake of the hoss. A hoss that's a bad actor is mighty like a mad dog. It has to be killed—or broke. So we break 'em. But now," he said, glancing toward the corrals, "I reckon you young ladies would like to pick out some nice gentle hosses to ride while you're here."

The girls nodded and crowded forward eagerly while Andy called to some of the cowboys who had been lingering enviously near.

"Bring out the sorrel and Nigger, will you, Jake?" he said to one of them. "I'll corral Lady and Nabob."

The girls watched with interest while the boys corraled the four horses Andy had selected and led them forth for the visitors' inspection.

They were splendid specimens of horse flesh, and for a moment the girls were simply lost in admiration. Nigger, as his name implied, was a magnificent coal-black animal without a speck of white upon him anywhere. He and Betty seemed to form a mutual admiration society on the instant, for with a gentle whinny he cantered up to the girl and began nosing inquisitively in her pocket in search of sugar. Luckily Betty had brought some with her, and she fed a couple of lumps to the beautiful animal, thereby definitely sealing their pact of friendship.

"Oh you, Nigger!" crooned Betty joyfully, as she rubbed the velvet muzzle. "You and I are going to be great little pals, aren't we? You perfect old darling!" And Nigger whinnied again and nosed about for more sugar.

"Well, I like that," cried Grace, breaking the silence in which they had all been enjoyably regarding the little scene. "Betty doesn't have to choose her horse—it chooses her."

"Oh well, Betty always did have a way with her," laughed Mollie, and promptly turned her attention to the remaining three horses.

"Lady" was a lovely white filly with whom Amy fell in love immediately.

"This one's mine," she cried, putting a possessive hand on Lady's flank while the latter turned her dainty head and regarded the girl out of softly-wistful brown eyes. "I wanted her as soon as I saw her."

Her claim was not disputed, for Grace was raving over the horse called Nabob, who was, by a strange coincidence, that very light tan color which she most adored.

"How did you know I always wanted a horse just like this?" she cried, turning joyfully to Andy Rawlinson who, with the other "boys" had been looking on amusedly.

"Well," drawled Andy, with a grin, "seems like you are all suited pretty well."

For Mollie, whose adventurous spirit craved a spice of the dangerous in everything, had taken immediately to the sorrel, who had apparently been given no name. He was a skittish horse, gentle, as Andy explained, but "pow'ful nervous—had to be sort o' coaxed along."

"You're my horse, all right," Mollie declared, stroking the animal's muzzle fearlessly, unmindful of rolling eyes and nervously twitching ears. "I don't like 'em too tame, old boy. And by the way," she added, struck by a sudden inspiration, "I've thought of just the name for you. I'm going to call you 'Old Nick.'"

And so, when the selection had been made, to everybody's satisfaction, nothing would do but the girls must try their mounts that very evening. They had brought their riding tags in preparation for their summer in the saddle, and when they had slipped into the tight breeches, and leather leggings, tailored coat, and snug fitting hat, they looked like what they were—four thoroughly modern and very pretty Outdoor Girls.

Later, when they rode proudly about the ranch on their splendid mounts, the ranch hands were lost in admiration of them.

"Gosh," said one, removing his hat and fanning himself with it, for the evening was warm, "when Andy said they was four girls comin' from the city to visit us I was plumb skeered. But these here girls, they ain't no ordinary kind, no siree. An' they sho' does know how to ride."

However, the girls were satisfied with a rather short ride that evening for they were out of practice and they knew that sore muscles would be the price of over-exertion.

In the days that followed they took longer and longer rides, even venturing along the rough forest trails when Andy Rawlinson was with them as guide and protector. Mr. and Mrs. Nelson rode, too, but, not being as strenuous as the girls, they were glad to have any one as capable as Andy Rawlinson to look out for their charges.

But one day, much as they liked him, the girls got a little tired of Andy's chaperonage, and at Mollie's suggestion they decided to "give him the slip."

"Anybody would think he was our granny, the way he dictates to us," she complained, as she flicked a fly from Old Nick's side, thereby causing him to shy wildly. "We know our way about all right now, and I'm sure we Outdoor Girls never needed anybody to look out for us, anyway."

"Hear, hear," laughed Betty, half way between conviction and protest. "I don't like to have Andy around all the time, any more than you do, Mollie, but I'm not sure that we know our way about as well as we might. If we should get lost——"

"Oh, don't be an old wet blanket," cried Mollie impatiently, and as Amy and Grace seemed for once to be of her mind, Betty had nothing to do but to surrender as gracefully as she could.

It was after lunch that the girls managed to slip away without being observed to where their mounts were tethered at the edge of the woodland. And oh, what a glorious sense of freedom when they were mounted and cantering down a cool forest trail—alone!

They had been this way with Andy before, so they had no fear of losing their path and they urged their horses to more and more speed, intoxicated by the sense of freedom.

What they did not notice was that the sun had disappeared behind an ominous bank of clouds and the wind was rising threateningly. And so they were caught fairly and squarely by the deluge that swept upon them with a bewildering suddenness.

Where to go? Where to turn for shelter from the driving rain and moaning wind? They checked their horses while they gazed at each other wildly.

Suddenly Betty's straining eyes made out what seemed to be the outline of a little shed or cabin, half hidden by surrounding foliage.

"There's a house over there," she cried, hastily dismounting and tying Nigger to a tree a little off the path. "Maybe whoever lives there will let us in till the rain stops."

The girls followed her example and hurriedly made their way on foot toward their one hope of refuge. When they reached the house

Betty started to knock, then paused uncertainly, her hand uplifted. For above the beat of the rain and the shrill whine of the wind came a strain of music, mournful, yet exquisitely beautiful. Amazed, forgetful of their discomfort, the girls listened while the throbbing, haunting melody wailed itself to a close.

"I—I've heard that music before," Betty murmured, then rapped gently, almost timidly, on the door.

CHAPTER VIII

ALONG THE TRAIL

Betty's knock had to be repeated twice before the occupant of the cabin responded.

"Knock harder, Betty, if——" Mollie was beginning when the door opened at last and a very strange person stood upon the threshold. Tall, with stooped shoulders and a head bent a little as though he had spent countless hours over his violin, with long, curly hair, and with the visioned eyes of the musician, the man was a figure that would have made people turn to stare at him anywhere.

"I—we—we are very sorry to trouble you," said Betty hesitatingly, as the musician made no effort to break the silence. "But it is raining hard, as you see, and we thought——"

The man started and frowned.

"Ah yes, of course," he said, moving aside and motioning them into the room. "You will find shelter here, but very little else, I fear."

As the girls entered rather hesitantly the man turned from them abruptly and, lifting the violin that lay upon the rough board table, he began with the utmost gentleness to put it in its case. The girls had the rather uncomfortable impression that the man was forcing himself to be polite to them—that if he had been any other than a gentleman he would have refused them admittance.

They looked uneasily at each other and then toward the one window in the room, and one thought was in the minds of all of them—to escape from the enforced hospitality of this man.

"I think the rain is letting up a little," said Grace softly.

"I reckon we won't have to stay more than a few minutes," agreed Betty, then, as their long-haired host put down his case and turned toward them, she ventured a shy compliment.

"We heard you playing as we came along," she said. "It was very wonderful."

"Thank you," said the man gruffly, and turned away so abruptly that Betty felt as if some one had struck her.

Mollie looked indignant and Amy put an arm about Betty as she whispered:

"The rain has nearly stopped, honey. Don't you think we had better go?"

So, with half-hearted expressions of thanks from the girls and no expression of regret at all from the man, the new acquaintances parted, the girls hurrying down the dripping path to where their horses were tethered.

Once Mollie looked back toward the cabin, and her indignation burst forth.

"Look, he could hardly wait for us to get outside to shut the door," she said. "Of all the ill-mannered——"

"Oh, I don't think he meant to be ill-mannered," interposed Betty mildly, as she reached Nigger and he whinnied a welcome. "He was just distantly polite, that's all. He didn't want to be bothered, probably, and he had a hard time to keep from showing it."

"Huh," grunted Mollie, as she flung herself upon Old Nick's back and patted him soothingly. "I'm sure he has some real reason for not wanting folks around. He acted mighty funny to me," she said.

"Goodness, hear the child!" cried Grace, as they rode swiftly back the way they had come through the fine drizzle. "She never can resist making a thief or something out of a perfectly ordinary person."

"Seems to me he is anything but ordinary," interposed Amy thoughtfully. "No ordinary person could play the violin the way he was playin it when we came up to the house. That sounded like the work of a master."

"Yes," agreed Betty, a faraway look in her eyes. "He plays exquisitely, if he does live in a little house away up in the woods. And I can't shake off the impression that I have heard that same selection played in just that same way somewhere before."

Though this first excursion had been somewhat of a failure, the girls were by no means discouraged and in the days that followed they rode almost constantly. Finally they began to know their way about like the natives.

Their rides were taken mostly in the open country, however, for in the woods they knew lurked very real dangers. But these they avoided more to save Mrs. Nelson worry than from any personal fears.

But one day, feeling more than usually adventurous and growing more and more confident of their ability to find their way around alone, they dared venture along a rocky trail that offered wonderful romantic opportunities.

"Oh, this is the life!" cried Grace, as Nabob stepped daintily over the rocks and underbrush that almost completely overgrew the narrow path. "A peach of a horse under you, the whole day before you, and nothing to do but enjoy yourself. Whoa-up there, Nabob. What's the matter with you?" for the horse had whinnied softly and shied almost imperceptibly to the side of the trail.

At the same time the other horses seemed to catch some of Nabob's uneasiness, and the girls were kept busy for the next few minutes soothing them and coaxing them back into a normal mode of progress.

"Something scared them," said Amy nervously. "Don't you think we had better go back, girls? This trail seems to be getting narrower and narrower. I don't believe anybody comes along here very often."

"Well, what of it?" cried Mollie sharply. "That's what we are here for, isn't it? If we wanted people, we could have plenty of them right back on the ranch."

"Stop quarreling, girls," said Betty, matter-of-factly. "We'll eat pretty soon and that will make everybody feel better." Kindly Mrs. Cummins had put up an appetizing lunch for the girls.

"Look!" she cried a moment later, as the trail broadened out and they reached a rather open space in the woods through which they could look straight down—for they were on a considerable elevation—into the thriving little mining town of Gold Run. "I didn't know you could see Gold Run from here."

"Doesn't it look funny and tiny?" cried Mollie, reining in beside her. "It must be an awfully long way off."

"Wouldn't this be a good place to eat?" queried Amy hopefully, and the girls laughed at her.

"We aren't hungry enough yet," said Betty, as she turned her horse to continue down the trail.

They rode on, following the trail as it wound deeper and deeper into the woodland, catching glimpses now and then of the mining camp down in the hollow.

It seemed as if they were really getting closer to Gold Run and, fascinated by the new game they were playing, forgetting their fears in the new sights and sounds all about them, the girls rode farther and farther into the heart of a forest, whose smiling face often served to hide some hideous danger.

But to the girls all was beauty and sunshine and they conversed merrily as they cantered along.

"When is Allen coming, Betty?" asked Grace. "I had an idea he would be here before this."

"Why, dad has written, asking him to come as soon as he can," answered Betty, striving to look unconscious. "You know what that girl Lizzie said about mother's relatives—she never knew she had them till she came here—and dad thinks some of these people may make up their minds to contest the will. They haven't made trouble yet—but you never can tell. Listen, girls," she added suddenly. "Will you promise not to breathe a word of it if I tell you a big secret?"

"Hope to die," they chorused piously.

"Well, our old friend Peter Levine has been around pestering mother again."

At this news, Grace, who was riding ahead, checked her mount so suddenly that Betty had all she could do to keep Nigger from swallowing Nabob's tail.

"For goodness' sake, put out your hand when you do that next time," laughed Betty.

"Well," said Grace as she gave Nabob a gentle slap that started him on again, "Peter Levine must want that ranch very badly, to be following us all over the continent this way."

"He seems to be rather anxious," said Betty dryly. "He has offered mother twenty thousand for it this time."

"Going up," cried Mollie, with a chuckle. "If your mother holds on much longer, Betty, she will be a millionaire."

"Well, mother is more certain than ever that there is something unusual about Gold Run Ranch," went on Betty, as she urged Nigger up a gentle slope. "She confidently expects to discover a gold mine, and so that's another reason why she thinks Allen ought to be here."

"Goodness, let's all get out and dig," cried Mollie.

"Can we have all we find, Betty?" called Amy, with a laugh.

"Every last gold brick," answered Betty happily, and then they came upon another open space, and there, lying not more than half a mile below them, was the mining town of Gold Run.

"Now here's the place to have some lunch," said Betty, slipping to the ground and leading Nigger off a little way into the woods where she tethered him securely. "We can look right down into the town and eat our lunch at the same time."

The girls followed suit, and it did not take them long afterward to discover that they were very hungry. So out came the lunch basket, and never did biscuits and cheese and fried chicken taste more delicious than they did to the girls right there in that romantic little spot in the woods.

"I hope it doesn't rain the way it did the other day," said Mollie, as she lazily surveyed a cloudless sky.

"We haven't even a cabin in the woods to go to this time," said Grace, adding, as the thought brought up a picture of the long-haired musician who had been so painfully polite: "I wonder what our friend, Long Hair, lives on, anyway. Maybe he goes out and kills bears and things. They say bear meat is very good eating," she added reflectively.

"Maybe we can catch one ourselves and take it home for dinner," suggested Mollie, and the girls looked as if they did not like her suggestion at all.

"Methinks the bear would be more likely to catch us," Betty was saying when a chorus of low whinnyings and stampings coming from where the horses were tethered caused them to jump to their feet in alarm. Suddenly the nervousness of the animals changed to panic and they began to rear and plunge, straining madly at the tethering straps, snorting and screaming with terror.

"Look!" cried Mollie, her voice shrilling above the noise. "There! In the woods! Oh, run for your lives, girls! Run!"

CHAPTER IX

DANGER AHEAD

Coming toward the girls through the trees, crouched low, sinister eyes fixed upon them, were two great timber wolves. The girls, terrified as they were, saw at a glance that it would be of no use to run, the movement would only infuriate the beasts and precipitate their attack.

"The trees!" gasped Betty, feeling herself in the grip of the deadly inertia that one experiences sometimes in a nightmare. "Make for the trees, girls; they are our only chance."

Luckily, the branches of the trees swung low to the ground, or the girls could never have saved themselves. As it was, they had barely time to swing themselves free of the ground when the great beasts darted into the open, fangs bared, snarling hideously. Then——

Bang! Bang! Two sharp reports from the direction of the woodland and one of the wolves sprang clear of the ground, then slunk into the underbrush, while the other staggered, fell, struggled to its feet, fell again, and after one convulsive movement, lay still.

While the girls stared, unable to follow this swift turn of events, there was the sound of running feet coming in their direction and the next moment two figures broke through into the cleared space.

One was a little wizened man who seemed, for all his apparent age, extremely agile. The other was a girl, a splendid, big creature, who stood as tall as the man, and who, like him, carried a rifle.

The two ran to the fallen animal, talking excitedly, and turned it over to be sure it was dead. They were so absorbed that they did not notice the girls, who dropped down quietly from their perches in the trees. The sight of the guns carried by the newcomers had had a tremendously reassuring effect upon them. The wonderful sensation of relief that swept over them as they realized their almost miraculous escape, was so keen as to be almost pain.

Still, they were not quite free from fear as they approached the prostrate body of the big beast, over which their rescuers were still bending. It was the girl who first discovered them.

"Hello!" she cried, straightening up and turning upon the girls a frank regard. "You was the ones this old boy was after, eh? Look, Dad," she added, pointing to where the four horses were still bucking and snorting in fright. "There's the hosses we heard, but I reckon 'twas these gals the wolves was after."

"I guess you're right," said Betty, trying to smile through a shiver. "It wasn't very much fun while it lasted, either."

At this the old man, who had very kindly, keen blue eyes in his seamed and wrinkled face, turned and spat upon the ground meditatively.

"You don't mean to tell me," he said, looking from one to the other of the girls, "that you purty young girls was out hyar all alone, without even a gun to protect yourselves with?"

"I guess we were." It was Mollie who spoke this time, and her tone was rueful. "We aren't used to this part of the world, you see, and so we didn't know what a risky thing we were doing."

"They are most as bad as the Hermit of Gold Run, aren't they, Dad?" asked the big girl, her eyes twinkling. "He goes about everywhere through the woods without a gun and only his violin for company; and, somehow or other, the beasts never molest him. Some says he charms 'em with his violin, but I think it's just luck," she added, with a wise shake of her head.

The girls, whose curiosity had revived as their fears subsided, listened with interest to this rather long speech of the mountain girl.

"Has this—er—hermit, as you call him——" Betty interrogated eagerly, "has he long curly hair and is he tall——"

"With stooped shoulders?" finished Amy.

The mountain girl looked amazed.

"Why yes. Do you know him?" she asked, adding, as though to explain her surprise: "He doesn't like to see people, you know, and folks round here don't know much about him 'cept that he plays the violin. That's why they calls him the hermit, 'cause he lives alone an' hates everybody."

"All except Meggy, here," interposed the old man, a look of pride in his eyes as he gazed at his daughter. "He likes her fust rate. She says it's 'cause she takes him grub an' good things to eat. But I know better."

80

"Pshaw, Dad," cried the girl, flushing with embarrassment. "It's jest one of your idees that people like me better'n most when they don't at all." As though to change the subject, she touched the stiff animal at her feet with the toe of her stout boot.

"What you aim to do with this one, Dad?" she asked. "It was your bullet got him. Mine went wild, an' I jest injured the other feller."

"Waal," said the old man, his gaze fixed speculatively on the big beast, "he's not wuth the trouble o' skinning an' his meat ain't much good, so I reckon we'd better leave him, daughter. Time I was gettin' back to the mine."

He turned to go, but Betty was before him, hand outstretched impulsively.

"Oh, but you must let us thank you," she cried. "If you and your daughter hadn't happened along just then I don't know what we should have done."

"Oh, thet's all right, thet's all right," said the old miner, too embarrassed to meet her eye. "Glad we could be some use to you, ma'am. But ef you'll take an old man's advice," he added, as he and his daughter started through the woods in the direction of Gold Run, "you won't go roaming around in these parts without a gun onto you. 'Tain't safe, noways."

"We won't," they promised.

Once their protectors were gone they were wild with impatience to get out of this place of dangers. Their fingers trembled as they untied the horses, and it was as much as they could do to get the animals to stand still long enough to mount them.

However, once in the saddle, they galloped[86] along that narrow trail at full speed, regardless of rocks and old stumps of trees and treacherous holes, their one thought to reach the open road—and safety.

When at last the plain stretched before them, level and red hot in the blazing afternoon sun, they all uttered a silent prayer of thankfulness.

"You were right, Amy," said Betty suddenly, as Amy came up abreast of her, "when you said the mountains could be cruel too."

"We'll not ever dare tell the folks," said Grace, shuddering at the memory of their close escape. "They would never let us out of their sight again."

"It was mighty lucky for us that Meggy and her father happened along just as they did," said Mollie. "I know I couldn't have held on very long where I was, and once on the ground I'd have made a lovely tender morsel for the little wolves."

"You flatter yourself," retorted Grace, and Amy shivered.

"I don't know how you girls can joke about such a thing," she said. "I was about frightened to death."

"I suppose you think the rest of us enjoyed it," said Mollie, and at this point Betty thought it was about time to interfere.

"Wasn't it odd—Meggy's speaking of our friend the musician and calling him the Hermit of Gold Run?" she said. "I'm glad the poor lonely fellow has a nice girl like Meggy to befriend him."

"Huh, he didn't seem to want befriending very much when we saw him," said Mollie. "We couldn't have been frozen more completely if we had dropped on an iceberg."

"Oh, well, he has 'ze temperament,'" said Grace, with an elaborate gesture.

"Seems kind of strange, his living up there all alone," said Amy thoughtfully. "You would think any one who could play the way he can would hate to bury himself in the wilderness. Unless——" she paused, and Mollie jumped joyfully into the opening.

"Unless there is some reason why he has to," said the latter, adding with an I-told-you-so air, "I thought there was some mystery about that man, and now you are beginning to think so yourselves. You just keep your eyes open and watch for a surprise!"

CHAPTER X

THE LANDSLIDE

After their perilous adventure, the Outdoor Girls shunned the forest unless they were accompanied by one or more of the cowboys at the ranch. Andy Rawlinson escorted them whenever he could, but his duties as foreman of the ranch kept him very busy and he sometimes appointed one of the ranch hands to take his place.

However, these excursions became less and less frequent as the girls became more interested in the booming mining town of Gold Run.

This they had visited with Mr. and Mrs. Nelson and Andy, and the whole thing made them feel more than ever as if they were living some motion picture drama.

There was the regulation general store and the inevitable dance hall where the lucky miners came to spend their golden nuggets and the unlucky tried to drown their misery in the companionship of others.

Their eyes wide with interest and pleasure and their tongues busy with questions, the girls cantered down the narrow, crooked wagon road called "Main Street." They read the names over the doors of the dingy little shops, commenting gayly upon their queerness.

"Peter Levine, Attorney," read Betty aloud from a sign just a little dingier than the rest. Then she drew rein and waited for her mother, who was riding more slowly with Mr. Nelson. The other girls, who had ridden on ahead, suddenly missed her, saw that she had stopped, and came back curiously.

"Look, Mother," Betty was saying as they came up. "This is where dear Peter Levine hails from. His checked suit and loud tie must look funny in that dingy little shop," she added, with a chuckle.

"Well, let's ride along," suggested Mrs. Nelson nervously. "He might see us and take it into his head to come out. And I don't want to have anything more to do with him until Allen comes."

"Allen," thought Betty, as they turned and cantered on again. "I wish he would hurry a little. He seems an awfully long time coming."

After they had seen all that there was to see of the town itself, Andy led them to some of the important mines on the outskirts. They listened with lively interest while the young fellow explained to them how the ore was extracted from the mountain side where it had lain unmolested for thousands of years.

"It almost seems a shame to disturb it," said Amy at this point, and the girls laughed at her.

"Just give me a chance at it, that's all," said Mollie longingly.

At one of these mines they met the old man and his daughter, Meggy, whose timely arrival a few days before had saved their lives. The two were in the midst of their work, the girl lifting and hauling with all the strength of a man, and they scarcely looked up as the party passed them, although the old man responded with a wave of his hand when Andy Rawlinson called to him.

"How's it goin', Dan?" asked the former.

"Oh, well enough, well enough," responded the man, with what seemed to the girls enforced cheerfulness. "We'll strike gold afore to-morrow, sure."

"Poor old Dan Higgins," said Andy, with a sobering of his good-natured face. "He's always goin' to strike gold 'to-morrow.' Sure, there's no one I'd rather see strike it rich than Dan an' that girl of his. But I'm 'fraid they're jest plumb unlucky. Funny thing, luck—and gold," he went on to soliloquize. "Some young fellers they come out here, thinkin' they can get back to the girl at home in a couple o' years with their pockets plumb full o' nuggets, an' instead, they toil their lives away till their hair grows white an' their skin gets crackly like parchment, an' never even a glimpse o' yellow. An' mebbe the feller next to him drills a hole three feet deep and he strikes a vein. Yes siree, if ever there was a real thing in this world, that thing is luck."

The girls were impressed and their hearts ached for Dan Higgins, his years of hope and work and his profitless mine. As for the girl, his daughter, Meggy——

"Are you sure Dan Higgins hasn't any chance of striking gold?" asked Betty, gravely.

"Not a bit of it," returned Andy Rawlinson quickly. "There's gold all around here—everybody thought Dan was mighty lucky when he staked out his claim. He may find gold yet. But," he added, and there was a fatalistic quality in his tone that chilled the girls, "you always have to reckon on luck."

In the days that followed it became quite the usual thing to see the Outdoor Girls, mounted on their splendid horses, galloping along the open road or cantering through the town of Gold Run. It was not long before they became general favorites in this country where girls of their type[92] were scarce, and the girls knew most of the rough but good-hearted miners by name. But perhaps of them all, their best and staunchest friends were old Dan Higgins and his daughter, Meggy.

The girls often visited the mine and were always greeted with the utmost heartiness by its owners. Once Betty had caught Meggy looking longingly at Nigger as he was trying his best to get some nourishment from the stubbly grass, and with the quick impulsiveness that was hers, she asked the girl if she would like a ride.

At the sudden radiance that flooded Meggy's face, Betty turned away abashed. She felt as though she had been given a glimpse of the girl's soul.

Meggy had her ride, and in the days that followed she had many others and the girl's fondness for Betty became almost worship. She liked the other girls, for they were always kind to her, but Betty was her idol.

"I have wanted all my life to own a horse," she confided to the Little Captain one day, as she stroked Nigger's shining coat with almost reverent fingers. "It would be the first thing I would buy for myself if dad should strike it rich." Her tone was brave, but the eyes that sought her father's toiling figure were sad. "Poor old dad," she said softly, "I don't think he would keep on any longer, if it wasn't for me."

On one of their visits to the mine the girls were astonished to find their mysterious musician there ahead of them. He seemed to be trying to help, but from where the girls watched unobserved, it looked as though he were more in the way than anything else.

Meggy was the first to discover them, and as she called out a greeting, the Hermit of Gold Run rose quickly to his feet and disappeared into the woods.

"Poor fellow," said Meggy, looking pityingly after him. "We let him try to help us because it seems to amuse him, but he really doesn't know how to work with his hands. His fingers were made for the fiddle."

"I certainly would like to find out more about that man," said Mollie, her forehead puckered into a puzzled frown. "He sure does act pretty funny."

"We'll have to visit him again some day," said Betty lightly, and then turned to question Meggy on the progress of the mine.

On their way home they took up the subject of the strange musician whose queer comings and goings had begun to be of more than usual interest to them.

"He acts—in a—a stealthy way," said Grace, striving for the exact words to express her meaning. "He positively sneaked away from us this morning. It seems to me people don't act like that unless they are afraid of something."

"He might just be afraid of people," Betty reminded her. "Or he may dislike people and want to be left alone. That would account for the name of 'hermit' that the natives around here have given him."

"But an ordinary hermit wouldn't be able to play like a virtuoso," objected Amy.

"Well, nobody said he was an ordinary hermit," retorted Mollie.

"To change the subject before you girls get to the hair-pulling stage," laughed Betty, as she turned Nigger's head toward the ranch, "I wish we could do something for Dan Higgins and Meggy. It's a shame for that splendid, loyal girl to have to spend all her youth, when she might be having good times like other girls, in doing the kind of work that's only fit for a man to do."

"And she's so brave about it, too," added Grace admiringly. "She keeps her head up like a thoroughbred."

"I've asked her to come over to the ranch," Betty went on thoughtfully. "She has a passion for horses, you know, and I told her we'd have Andy Rawlinson pick her out a beauty from the corrals. I could see that she was awfully tempted, but she said no, she couldn't leave her father."

"Probably the real reason she refused was because she hadn't decent clothes to wear," said Mollie sagaciously. "The poor girl is almost in rags."

"I wish we could help," sighed Betty. "But she and her father are proud, like most of the other people around here. They just have to stand on their own feet."

"I wonder if they have enough to eat," mused Amy. "It would be dreadful to think of them actually hungry."

"Oh, I guess there's no danger of that," said Mollie. "As long as there are wild animals in the woods and Dan Higgins and Meggy have guns they won't starve to death."

"And maybe they really will find gold, anyway," said Grace hopefully.

They rode along silently for a while. In their abstraction they had taken the long way home, instead of cutting directly across the ranch in the direction of the house. They were on a rather narrow trail, so narrow, that they could not ride two abreast but were strung out in single file, Indian fashion. On one side of them rose the mountain, huge and majestic, and on the other was a sheer drop of a hundred feet or so into a rocky canyon.

The girls had always loved this ride because of the wonderful view it afforded them of the surrounding country. But that very morning Dan Higgins had warned them not to go that way.

"The mountain is pow'ful oncertain," the old man had told them. "Part of it is apt to fall on you any time if you get too close to it."

Betty thought of this warning, but too late. An ominous rumbling jerked her eyes upward and she saw a sight that almost froze the blood in her veins. It seemed indeed to her terrified fancy as if the whole mountain were falling upon them. A great mass of dirt and brush and rock was hurtling down upon them with sickening velocity. A landslide—and they were directly in its path!

CHAPTER XI

IN THE CAVE

Luck was with the Outdoor Girls that day—or fate—call it what you will. In the side of the mountain close to where they were, had been drilled a hole forming a large, artificial cave—probably the work of some miner who had abandoned operations almost at the beginning either from lack of funds or ambition.

Into this hole the girls dashed, driven on by their frightful peril. Amy was the last to enter, and she had barely urged her nervous little filly into the opening when, with a terrific rumbling and rattling, the mass of earth and stones fell, covering the mouth of the cave and leaving them in such absolute darkness that it seemed as if they must suddenly have been stricken blind.

"Oh! oh!" moaned Amy, her trembling hand striving vainly to quiet the frightened animal under her. "We're buried alive, girls, we're buried alive! We'll never get out of this—never!"

"Please stop that, Amy," Betty's voice came out of the darkness, harsh, unnatural, like the crack of a whip. "The only danger we're in is the danger of losing our heads. Whoa, there, Nigger, old boy. Take it easy, beauty—there's nothing to be frightened about—there—there——" and she crooned to the big beast soothingly.

Someway, the other girls managed to follow her example, enough at least to quiet their restless mounts. Grace was sobbing, more from nervousness than fright, but she managed to say with a catch in her breath, "Stand still, Nabob—don't be such a s-silly. Isn't your Auntie Grace here with you?"

But it was Mollie who had the real problem. For while "Old Nick's" skittishness was more amusing than dangerous in the open, here, in this small place, with the other horses already difficult to manage, any real panic on his part would be more than likely to precipitate a real tragedy.

In the dark, unable to see a foot before their faces, only the power of their wills to prevent a stampede of their panicky horses which would mean death to them all and, worst of all, the possibility of smothering or starving to death in this walled-in cave! This was the appalling situation which confronted the four Outdoor Girls.

Mollie, her teeth grimly set, her knees dug into Old Nick's sides, was doing her best to keep him from trying to climb on the back of one of the other horses.

"Oh, Mollie, make him stop it," cried Amy frantically. "He'll kill poor Lady. Make him stop!"

"What do you suppose I'm trying to do," gritted Mollie between clenched teeth. "Do you think I like riding the side of a wall? Get down there, Old Nick, you wicked beast. Just wait till I get you outside."

Although this threat was uttered sternly, Mollie had never been nearer to crying in her life. Luckily, a cruel dig of her spurs in the horse's side brought the big beast to his senses. He dropped to the ground and stood there, quivering in every muscle and nickering plaintively.

"Good work, Mollie, old girl," cried Betty's voice encouragingly, and Mollie, wiping a tell-tale drop from the corner of her nose, answered in a voice that held never a quiver: "I couldn't fail you, Little Captain. Not at a time like this," and then she felt very brave and heroic.

The horses were quiet, huddled together at the farther end of the cave as though they found comfort in company, and thus one great danger was passed. But the girls had still the other and greater one to face.

"We'd better dismount," said Betty's voice, surprisingly calm and matter-of-fact. It was this ability of Betty Nelson's to keep her nerve and her head in any difficulty, to see almost at a glance the best thing to do and the best way to do it, that had led the girls to call her their Little Captain. And now as they listened to her cool voice, directing them as always in an emergency, some of her self-control communicated itself to them and they followed her leadership without question.

"The horses will stand quietly now, I think," she said, and swung herself cautiously from Nigger's tall back and felt her way slowly past the horses, out to the small open space between them and what had once been the mouth of the cave.

The girls followed her example, the horses making no protest, save to whinny anxiously and crowd a little closer together.

"Where are you, Betty?" cried Grace plaintively, stubbing her toe on a stone and emitting an injured "ouch."

"I'm over here," responded Betty reassuringly. "Stretch out your hand and I'll grab it."

"Oh, for a match, my kingdom for a match!" said Mollie, brushing her hand across her eyes as though to relieve them of the weight of that terrific darkness. "Why aren't we men so we could carry 'em in our pockets—the matches I mean, not the men," she added with a chuckle that ended in a sob.

"Well, here we are," said Grace, when they had found each other in the inky blackness. "Now you've got us, Betty, what are you going to do with us?"

"I don't know—yet," responded Betty honestly. "I guess we've got to talk it over and decide what it is best to do."

Amy groaned.

"Meanwhile we smother," she said.

"Nonsense," retorted Betty briskly. "There's enough air in this place to keep us alive for twenty-four hours at least."

"Twenty-four hours," protested Amy, the panic she had felt at the first threatening to overwhelm her again. "But, Betty, there isn't a chance in the world that anybody will come along here in the next twenty-four hours."

"That's right, too," agreed Mollie, a prickly sensation of pure fright tickling the roots of her hair. "Dan Higgins said this trail was practically never used because of the danger from the mountain. This is a pretty pickle, this is!"

"And even if anybody should come along," Grace pointed out gloomily, "they couldn't be expected to guess that there are four girls and four horses buried in this hole in the wall."

"And I don't believe we could ever in the world make ourselves heard through that mass of rocks and dirt," added Mollie. "Looks as though we had just about come to the end of our rope, I should say."

Amy began to cry again softly, and Betty, who had been listening with increasing irritation to this conversation, burst forth indignantly:

"Of all the silly things I ever heard!" she denounced them hotly, "I think you girls are the worst. You seem to forget that you are Outdoor Girls and that we have been in a good many tight places that were almost as bad as this. Why, we can't expect to have good times and adventures without once in a while getting the worst of it. If this is the way you are going to take a little bad luck," she finished her tirade in a fury that whipped the girls like a lash, "then I'm through, that's all. I refuse to be one of four Outdoor Girls that don't deserve the name."

She paused, and the girls were silent for a moment, feeling a little dazed. The tongue-lashing had been just what they needed, as Betty very well knew. It made them angry.

"Oh well," said Mollie sullenly, "if you are so much better than the rest of us, Betty, perhaps you can tell us what to do. I'm sure we would be just as glad to get out of this as you."

"Then help me think of some way to do it," Betty retorted, more quietly. "Surely we can't accomplish it by making up our minds ahead of time that we are doomed."

"Suppose you suggest something, yourself," said Grace resentfully.

"All right," said Betty, whose quick mind had been working busily. "I am as sure as you girls are that the possibility of rescue from anybody outside is slight. Of course," she added breathlessly, "when we don't come home dad and mother would become worried and start a search party."

"They wouldn't miss us before night though," said Grace.

"Exactly," Betty caught her up. "And at night they wouldn't be as apt to discover the landslide as they would in the daylight. They would naturally think of the woods first. But the next day, anybody familiar with the trail would be sure to notice that there had been a landslide and they would be almost sure to connect it with us——"

"But Betty," wailed Grace, forgetting that a moment before she had been angry with the Little Captain, "all that is just supposition, and you know as well as we do that we are likely not to be discovered until—until——"

"It's too late," finished Mollie. "Why don't you say it? It's the truth."

"And since it is the truth," Betty took her up briskly, "there is all the more reason why we should take things in our own hands and work out our own salvation."

Betty impatiently cut short Amy's discouraged "How?"

"Now listen," she said. "There are plenty of stones in this cave——"

"My toes cry aloud that they know it," interjected Grace, but no one laughed—they were too intent upon Betty. They were beginning to realize what she had in mind, and the realization brought a thrill of hope.

"If we could find any sharp enough—stones I mean," Betty went on, "we might use them as a sort of shovel and try to dig our way out. Of course," she added, as the girls began to grope eagerly among the dirt and débris at their feet for stones sharp enough to answer the purpose, "the mouth of the cave may be choked up too solidly with dirt and underbrush and things for us to get through. But in that case we'd just have to think up some other way, that's all."

"I've got a peach," cried Mollie slangily, as her hand struck a big stone sharp enough to serve her purpose. "I ought to be able to dig my way through the side of a house with this fellow."

"And here's the very one that got too familiar with my toe," said Grace, as she picked up another serviceable stone. "I'm going to get even with it now. I shall make it work as it never worked before."

After much groping and knocking of heads together, Betty and Amy also armed themselves with imitation shovels, and so the work began.

And it was work indeed. For what seemed hours to the anxious girls they toiled, digging sometimes with the stones, sometimes in desperation with their hands until it seemed to them they must have dug their way half through the mountainside. And still that blank wall of dirt, that impenetrable darkness, that stubborn barrier between them and the blessed sunshine. Amy was the first to give way.

She sank back on the dank floor of the cave and buried her face in her dirt-stained hands.

"We'll never get out of here!" she sobbed. "And I'm st-starving to d-death!"

CHAPTER XII

IN THE DARKNESS

Now the girls had been hungry before the accident occurred and, it being several hours since then, they were, by this time, as any one could readily see, in a rather bad state. Therefore, Amy's complaint was very unfortunate and, had it not been for Betty, it might have ruined the morale of the girls completely.

"Good gracious, Amy, don't talk about starving to death," cried Mollie, dismayed. "That's coming too near the truth for comfort. Oh, this miserable stone. It's cutting clear through my hand!"

"And my back is nearly broken," said Grace, adding, as she turned ferociously upon the still-sobbing Amy: "Stop that crying, Amy Blackford. Don't you know it is catching?" and a suspicious break at the end of her sentence, proved the truth of the assertion.

"Girls, please don't," begged Betty, still digging automatically at the stubborn wall of stones and dirt. "If you all begin to cry, then we might just as well throw up our hands and say we are beaten."

It was not long after that that the girls found what they called their "second wind." They forgot that they were ravenous, that their backs ached and that their hands were scratched and torn. They worked furiously in the darkness, their goal the out-of-doors they loved so well.

For a long time they did not notice that the air was becoming very close and oppressive and that the perspiration that bothered them so was caused not alone by their exertion. And when the realization did come it had the effect of goading them on to more furious effort.

That the horses also felt the change in the atmosphere, was attested to by their increased nervousness. The trampling of their hoofs sounded ominous to the girls—they made queer little puffing noises as if they were getting their breath with greater and greater difficulty.

In one terrible instant the girls realized what might happen when what was discomfort to the animals now, should become torture. Maddened by pain and fright, it would be no longer possible to quiet them. And then—and then——

"Don't you think we'd better stop and try to quiet the horses?" asked Mollie once, as the champing and snorting in the blackness behind them became more marked.

"I don't think it would do any good," Betty answered between clenched teeth as she scooped and dug, scooped and dug. "Better keep on working, girls. It's the one chance we have."

Oh, the horror of it, the nightmare of it! The heavy air, the hideous dark, the nervous trampling of those death-bearing hoofs—— The girls spoke no longer. They were beyond speech. Almost maddened by terror themselves, they scooped and dug, scooped and dug——

Once they thought they heard voices outside, and shrilly they cried to their imaginary rescuers. No answering "hallo" reached them, and the only effect of their cries seemed to be to add to the fright of their horses and so endanger themselves still more.

On, on, on—while their aching muscles seemed to grow numb with the strain and their lungs nearly burst with the pressure upon them.

At last they gave in—it seemed that they had to give in. All except Betty, who kept on desperately, doggedly, her muscles barely able to respond to the last call she was making upon them.

"I can't go on any more. I'm all in," said Mollie, a desperate quiet in her voice. "My arms are like lead and my hands are so numb I can' feel the stone. I guess this is the last adventure of the Outdoor Girls. We have just had one too many, that's all."

"Oh, Mollie!" Betty drew in a labored breath that caught on a sob. "Please don't give up—please! I've counted on you— — " she paused, jerked her head up, her attention turned on the spot where her hand still automatically dug at the earth.

She sniffed, experimentally, sniffed again, stilling the wild throb of hope that was almost a pain at her heart.

"What is it, Betty, what is it?" cried Mollie, sensing something strange. Amy and Grace fought off the dizziness that was stealing over them and leaned forward.

But Betty had jumped to her feet, had dropped the stone and was tearing with her bare hands at that thin place—that thin place— — It gave under her mad onslaught, and suddenly her hand slipped through into the air—the air— — A breath of it swept into her tortured lungs, and she leaned there, laughing, crying, the tears of sheer weakness running down her dirt-stained face.

"Girls!" she babbled, "out there is the air—the good old air—enough of it for all of us! We're saved, do you hear? We're saved!"

Exhausted as they were, the girls tore at the tiny hole that Betty had made until there was an opening big enough for them to crawl through.

And oh! the indescribable ecstasy of it, the joy of it, just to lie there, trembling with weakness, and drink in great drafts of that life-giving air, thinking of nothing, caring for nothing but that they were alive there in their great out-of-doors. One never comes really to appreciate life until one has been close to death.

It was a long time before they ventured to go on. They had not realized how near exhaustion they had been until the tension had relaxed. When at last they did start for home, on foot, they were still trembling and they dared not glance down the canyon at their right for fear of becoming dizzy.

They had been long hours in the cave, and when they finally left the trail and cut across the plain toward the ranch it was nearly dark. They did not realize the startling sight they must present to any one who might not know of their plight until they met Andy Rawlinson and some other boys from the ranch starting out to search for them.

At sight of the mud-stained, blood-stained Outdoor Girls, Andy Rawlinson fairly tumbled from his pony and came running toward them while the other boys stood agape.

"What in the world——" began Andy, but Betty stopped him with a weary gesture. As briefly as she could she told him what had happened and asked him to go back and get their horses.

"It's getting pretty dark now, you know," she reminded him, when he seemed inclined to linger and ask questions. "Soon you won't be able to see what you're doing. Won't you please hurry?"

"Surest thing you know," responded the boy quickly, his nice eyes full of sympathy for them. "Some of the boys will see you home—your folks are getting awfully worried about you, you know—and the rest of us will go on and dig out the poor bronchos. So long. We'll be back pronto."

"And now home," sighed Betty, as she looked at the ranch house just visible in the distance. "And a bath—and something to eat. What does that sound like, girls?"

"Heaven!" they answered.

CHAPTER XIII

THE LURE OF GOLD

The task of releasing the imprisoned horses was not such an easy task as the girls and even Andy Rawlinson had thought it would be.

In the first place, it took Andy and his company some time to discover the place along the trail where the landslide had occurred, for Betty's account had been hasty and excited and she had overlooked several details that might have helped them in their work.

And when they did reach the scene of what might have been a tragedy the ranch hands were appalled by the immensity of the landslide. There had been several small ones in that vicinity, but this was what Andy termed a "humdinger."

There was a stamping and snorting from inside that dirt-choked cavern that, there in that lonely spot on the very edge of night, seemed positively uncanny to the men who stood and listened.

"Better get busy, boys," said Andy suddenly. "Those hosses ain't goin' to get any easier in they minds an' it's about time we dug 'em out of there. Back to Gold Run as fast as we can get there for the right kind of tools from the miners. We may need some more men, too. Gosh, but I didn't know it was as bad as that," he added with a glance over his shoulder as he turned his pony and dashed back down the trail in the direction of Gold Run. "Reckon 'twas just plain grit that got those girls out."

Back in Gold Run they found several miners who were willing to offer both themselves and their tools toward the work of liberation, and soon the cowboys returned, accompanied by men with lanterns, and fell to work with a will.

Two hours later, Andy Rawlinson ventured into the blackness of the cave, swinging his lantern before him, and led forth the first of the frightened horses.

Meanwhile the girls had bathed away the stains of their adventure, and after a hearty meal cooked by an over solicitous "Miz Cummins" and served by a frankly envious and inquisitive Lizzie, they felt considerably more like their old self-confident selves.

However, they begged not to have to go to bed, as Mrs. Nelson anxiously suggested, until the boys had returned with their horses.

"I'm beginning to get dreadfully worried," Betty confessed after an interval of staring out into the darkness. They were on the biggest of the many porches boasted by the quaint old ranch house, waiting eagerly for the first sound that would announce the return of Andy and the others with their horses.

"I'd never get over it if anything happened to Old Nick," said Mollie, taking up Betty's theme. "Maybe we'd better borrow some other horses from the corral and follow them."

"You'll do nothing of the kind," said Mr. Nelson, his voice sounding unusually stern there in the darkness. "I am going to keep my eye on you for the rest of to-day, at least!"

And so they contented themselves as well as they could with waiting and finally were rewarded by the regular beat of galloping horses in the distance.

"They're coming!" cried Betty, springing to her feet, then turned to her father pleadingly: "You won't mind if we go down to meet them, will you, Dad?" she asked. "They are our chums, you know—the horses, I mean."

Mr. Nelson nodded, and down the steps the girls sprang, racing out to meet that sound of galloping hoofs which was coming ever nearer. A few minutes later they were caressing the nervous animals that had gone with them into the very shadow of death, rubbing their noses, laughing and crying over them and calling them endearing names till it's a wonder the cowboys, who stood by, grinning sympathetically, did not turn green with envy.

"Some anymiles do have all the luck," said one of them.

After that the girls and their horses were almost inseparable. If left to themselves, the latter would follow the girls around like dogs. Even "Old Nick," who had been the most difficult to understand and win, now was devoted to Mollie. She was the only one who could quiet him, and though there were some who did not care to ride him because of his skittishness, he was never anything but gentle and docile with her.

As the days passed the girls became more and more interested in Meggy Higgins until the longing to give her one good time, in spite of her pride, became almost an obsession with them.

One day Betty begged so hard that the girl finally consented to take a holiday and go out with them for a day's fun. But Meggy surrendered reluctantly, in spite of the fact that this invitation of the girls had been like a glimpse of wonderland to her.

"I reckon dad can get along one day without me, specially as the hermit can do part of my work. Pa's broke him in so he can be real helpful now——"

But she got no farther, for Betty threw her arms around the surprised girl and hugged her happily.

"I'm awfully glad!" she cried, adding with eyes that sparkled: "I tell you what I'll do. I'll let you ride Nigger. There's a darling little brown colt over at the ranch that I've been just dying to try out."

Sudden tears sprang to Meggy's eyes, and with the disgust of all mountain folk for the expression of sentiment, she turned away impatiently to hide this tell-tale sign of weakness. But Betty had glimpsed the tears and she was satisfied.

The day was all that even Meggy Higgins' starved imagination could have expected of it. The miner's daughter was so beatifically happy that the girls found a new and most satisfying thrill in her enjoyment.

All her short, work-driven life Meggy Higgins had wanted a horse, a beautiful, sleek animal with supple limbs and shining coat like the one that she was riding now—Betty's Nigger. Many have desired a fortune, some political fame, others social position, but Meggy merely desired a horse. And even this had been denied her because her father had been dazzled by the lure of gold, a fortune always just before his eyes, but never to be grasped.

The girls were sorry for old Dan Higgins and his thwarted hopes. But they were infinitely more sorry for this girl of his to whom hardship was a daily reality and pleasure a golden vision to be indulged in only by girls whose fathers did not own a worthless claim.

"Sometimes," spoke up Mollie, as she reined Old Nick into a walk, "I wish I had the courage to rob somebody else's mine, Meggy, and plant the gold in yours. It doesn't seem fair for you to work all the time and get nothing for it."

The girl smiled sadly.

"I'm used to that," she said, with a grim philosophy far beyond her years. Then she added, with a quick loyalty that made the girls' hearts warm to her: "I don't mind. I'd do anything for dad an' I guess if he thought I was gettin' discouraged he'd jest plum up an' quit. He's gittin' old, he is, an' he ain't that spry like he used to be. All he has is his hope in that mine—an' me. Ef you killed that you might as well kill him."

After a while they stopped in the shade of some stunted trees and had lunch. The girls could tell from Meggy's popping eyes that the delicacies they drew forth from Miz Cummins'[lunch basket had never been dreamed of in all her hum-drum, joyless life.

Tongue sandwiches, buttered corn-bread, fried chicken that you were at perfect liberty to take up in your fingers and nibble to your heart's content, jelly and olives and hot cocoa in the thermos bottle with rich cream already in it—truly a feast even worthy of the Outdoor Girls!

After lunch the girls strolled around a bit, leaving their mounts to graze lazily. They talked of many things, the adventures they had had, the curious people they had met in their adventuring, while Meggy listened to it all, drinking it in thirstily.

"To think of all the things you've seen," she breathed at last. "An' I've spent all my time sence I was able to toddle, I reckon, betwixt our cabin an' the mine—back an' forth, back an' forth——"

After that they rode on again and it was quite late in the day when they decided it was time to be going back.

"I don't see," said Grace, as they neared the ranch, "why we don't lay out some claims and start digging ourselves, girls. The north end of this ranch is quite near the other mines. We might strike gold."

The words were spoken laughingly, but Meggy took them seriously.

"Mebbe there's some truth in that," she said soberly. "Dad allus reckoned they might be gold on Gold Run Ranch."

A short time later they left her at the mine and Betty mounted Nigger, leading the brown colt by the reins. Meggy had tried to stammer some words of thanks, but the girls would have none of it. They waved to her gayly and started for home.

After an unusually long and thoughtful silence, Amy spoke up softly.

"Betty," she said, "if Meggy is right about the ranch, there being gold here, I mean, then what your mother had thought all along may turn out to be the truth."

"Well," said Betty, a joyous lilt to her voice that the girls knew well, "Allen will be here in a few days and then we'll start our gold hunt. Gold!" she repeated softy. "There is something romantic in the very sound of it!"

CHAPTER XIV

A DISCOVERY

Up to this time the weather had been remarkably fine, but on this particular morning the Outdoor Girls woke to find that the sky was overcast and there was every indication of a stormy day.

"Oh bother," grumbled Mollie, as after their breakfast she gloomily surveyed the landscape from the cretonne-curtained window. "Just as I was about to suggest a real adventure, too!"

"What do you mean—'real adventure?'" queried Grace, lazily. The day before she had bought a new box of candy and a magazine, and so it happened that she was the only one of the four of them who really did not care whether it rained or not.

Mollie turned from the window and regarded them resentfully. Then she looked more hopeful as her eyes rested on Betty, who was sorting the contents of a too-crowded dresser drawer.

"You are with me, anyway, aren't you, Betty?" she asked, almost wistfully. "We'll leave these other two at home, and you and I will go on our adventure."

"All right," said Betty, with a lack of enthusiasm that fell with a dampening effect upon Mollie's ears. The disastrous quality of their last adventure had had a dampening effect on the girls' enthusiasm for this form of entertainment, and for the present they preferred the safety of the ranch to the lure of the great unknown, as it were. However, this condition of mind was only temporary. They would soon be as eager as ever for new experiences. "I'm game for anything, Mollie dear, as long as you keep away from land-slides and wild animals."

"Just hear the child!" said Mollie disgustedly. "As if an adventure would be an adventure without a little danger mixed in!"

"Just what is your great idea, Mollie?" asked Betty mildly. Mollie was beginning to glower. And if somebody did not stop her at the beginning, there was sure to be a fracas. Betty knew this from experience. "Suppose you tell us about it and get it out of your system. As I said before, I'm willing to do anything if it isn't hunting lions and tigers."

Mollie grunted disgustedly.

"Well, there isn't a thing really exciting about it, if that's what you mean," she said. "I just thought that since we had nothing special to do to-day we might visit the Hermit of Gold Run again. We might be able to solve the mystery about him in some way," she added as a special inducement, since the girls still seemed unenthusiastic.

Grace laughed indulgently.

"Just how do you expect to solve this mystery?" she asked, with a giggle. "You certainly can't do it by looking at him."

"Oh well, if that's the way you feel," retorted Mollie, feeling very much abused, "I'm sorry I spoke about it. Only I thought we had already decided to pay him a visit."

"And so we had," said Betty, closing the dresser _drawer_ with a bang and coming unexpectedly to her aid. "And I, for one, am with you in that, Mollie. I have felt from the first," she went on earnestly, while Mollie regarded her with growing hope, "that I had not only heard the selection that that man played but that I had seen him somewhere before—quite a long time ago."

Impressed by Betty's earnestness, Grace had laid down her magazine and Amy was becoming interested.

"I know it's ridiculous," Betty continued, as though to justify herself, "but I can't help feeling that way, just the same."

"That thing he played sounded familiar to me, too," Grace admitted, now entirely abandoning her magazine and sitting up. "It has been haunting me ever since we heard him playing that day, and yet I can't think of the name of it."

Softly Amy began to hum a popular song, but Mollie interrupted her impatiently.

"Well then, since you all feel that way about it," she said eagerly, "I don't see why it wouldn't be fun to scout around his cabin a little bit and see if we can't pick up some information. I'm really curious about him."

"All right, let's," said Betty, with the decision for which she was famed. "Get your riding togs on, girls, and we'll play detective."

This time it was Mollie who held back.

"How about the weather?" she demurred. "Looks as if we were likely to get wet."

"Who cares?" said Betty airily, adding, as she stopped at the door to make them a little bow: "It would give us an excuse to see His Highness again."

Half an hour later they had saddled their ponies and were cantering off briskly to visit the Hermit of Gold Run.

"Aren't you a little bit afraid to go in there?" asked Amy, reining in as they reached the narrow trail through the woods that led near the musician's cabin. "We might run into some wolves, as we did that other time."

"We were much further in the woods than the Hermit's cabin," said Mollie impatiently. "And it was in an entirely different direction, too. Go ahead, silly, or I'll ride right over you," and as she was urging Old Nick forward until he crowded uncomfortably against the little white filly, Amy had no other course but to do as she was bid.

Nevertheless, she was not the only one who was uneasy, and it might have been observed that the girls glanced often into the shadows of the underbrush on either side of the narrow trail.

There were wild animals in that forest, as they had good reason to know, and though they seldom ventured this close to civilization, still there was no use in tempting fate!

"I didn't know it was as far in as this," said Grace, after they had ridden some distance in silence. "Are you sure we haven't passed the cabin, Betty?"

"Why, we aren't nearly there yet," was Betty's discomforting reply. "It's quite a way beyond that next turn in the trail."

Grace said nothing, but she gripped the reins harder in her hands. She had made up her mind that at the first sign of danger she would turn Nabob and make a dash back down the trail for safety.

After that the silence became so pronounced that Mollie noticed it and laughed nervously.

"Why all the noise?" she asked jocosely. "It nearly breaks my ear drums."

"Hush," cried Amy warningly. "I thought I heard something."

"That was your own heart hammering against the tree trunks," retorted Mollie dryly, at which the girls giggled and the tension relaxed.

"Let's talk about something nice," Betty suggested. "Gold, for instance."

"Or Allen," teased Grace. "I reckon you won't be glad or anything when he gets here."

"I guess mother will be gladder than any of us," replied Betty promptly, trying to shift the spotlight from herself. "She was so excited when I told her what Dan Higgins said about the possibility of there being gold on the ranch that she hardly closed her eyes all night. I told her she was getting to be a regular adventuress."

"Like her daughter," said Mollie, with a chuckle.

"Just think of the story we can tell the boys when we get home," said Amy rapturously, adding apologetically as the girls glanced at her: "If we find the gold, I mean."

"Listen to the child!" cried Betty gayly, while the other girls laughed. "And we huven't begun lo dig yet. I told your horses, Amy dear, hold your horses."

They did this very thing literally the next moment, for they came in sight of the queer little cabin of the man whom the natives called the Hermit of Gold Run.

Quickly they jumped down, tethered the horses as they had done before on the day when they had first made the acquaintance of this remarkable man, and started rather hesitantly down the path toward the house.

As they came nearer the haunting strains of the music that had puzzled them before once more floated out through the open windows and they paused, lost once again in the spell of it.

The music stopped, and they went on, hardly knowing what their next move was to be, yet drawn irresistibly by their curiosity. Then once more they heard the violin, but evidently the mood of the player had changed. The melody fraught with pathos, wailing, pleading, no longer reached them. The theme had changed—light, airy, sparkling, it reminded the girls of fairies dancing on the grass in the moonlight.

Mollie grasped Betty's arm.

"I know that!" she cried excitedly. "It's something of Chopin's, a nocturne, I think. Girls, I know where I heard that selection played just that way before."

They gazed at her, their eyes asking the question before their lips could form it.

"At the Hostess House!" cried Mollie. "Don't you remember that concert we gave with some of the great artists?"

"That big benefit!" cried Betty excitedly. "You've got it, Mollie! That's what I was trying to think of!"

"Sh-h," said Grace, a finger to her lips. "He has stopped playing. He may hear us."

"All right," said Betty. "Let's get back to the trail where we can talk this thing over."

They did not stop at the trail, however, for some memory of the danger lurking in the woods drove them out on to the main road where they might talk in peace.

"Now then," said Betty eagerly, as they reached the road, crowding their horses close together and reining them in to a walk. "What do you make of this, girls? If this man is really one of those artists that played at that big concert, then he is famous and there is something more than strange in his hiding up here in the woods."

"Goodness, we don't need anybody to tell us that," said Grace. "He certainly must be in hiding for something he's done—unless he has been disappointed in love," she added sentimentally.

"I don't believe he was ever in love with anything but his violin," said Mollie.

"Can't somebody think of the name of the violinist that played at the benefit?" asked Betty, who had been trying for some minutes past to accomplish that very thing.

"It was something like Croup, I think," said Mollie, wrinkling her forehead.

"Goodness, how romantic," said Grace, with a laugh.

"I tell you how we can find out the name," said Amy suddenly.

"How?" they questioned.

"I think I have a program, and I can send home for it," said Amy.

"Good girl!" cried Mollie, slapping her on the back with a violence that nearly threw her from Lady's back and caused that gentle little animal to turn her head inquiringly. "We little thought we had a genius in our midst!"

CHAPTER XV

ALLEN ARRIVES

Amy was delighted with the praise she received from the girls and the first thing she did after they returned to the ranch was to write home to her guardian for the concert program she had so luckily saved.

Naturally the girls were more curious than ever after this second trip to his little cabin in the woods and longed to find out about this strange musician who hid himself so persistently from the world.

"Of course," Grace said, during one of the many times when they talked the matter over, "we're not at all sure that the Hermit is the same man who played at our benefit."

"Of course we're not," Mollie agreed with her. "There must be a great many musicians who can play those same selections that we heard him play."

"That's all very true," said Betty argumentatively. "But if he is really this same musician that played at our benefit, then that explains the queer hunch I've had of having seen him somewhere before."

"Well," said Mollie resignedly, "I guess all we can do for the present is to wait until Amy gets her program. When we find out the name of the violinist that played for us then we can decide what to do next about the Hermit."

Reluctantly they admitted that what she said was true, and for the time being let the discussion rest there.

Then came the day when Betty received a letter from Allen announcing that he would reach Gold Run the following afternoon on the four-thirty-five train. The letter ended by begging her to meet the train herself and please not to send any one else, for no one else would do!

Betty's pretty face flushed a deeper pink and her eyes shone brighter as she read this passage—and two or three others—several times over. Then she went to find the girls and tell them the good news.

They also had received mail from the other boys and some of the folks at home, and she found them all together on the eastern porch having the time of their lives. Mollie and Amy were perched on the railing while Grace and a box of candy reposed in a hammock.

"Well, have you finished reading yours already?" Mollie greeted the Little Captain as she swung up the steps. "It was such a fat one I thought it would take you till lunch time at least to get through with it."

"Speak for yourself," retorted Betty, too happy to mind being teased. "Guess what, girls!" she added, unable to keep the news to herself for another minute, "Allen arrives via the Western Limited at four-thirty or thereabouts to-morrow afternoon."

"Hooray!" cried the girls, and momentarily forgot their own letters in very real delight. Allen Washburn was a favorite with all of them.

"Will you let us all go to meet him, Betty dear?" asked Grace, with a twinkling smile. "Or does he insist on seeing you alone?"

"Don't be silly," retorted Betty good-naturedly. "I know he would take it as a personal slight if you weren't all there to welcome him."

"Well, I don't know," Mollie commented ruefully. "Something tells me he would manage to live through it even if we weren't there. But go on, Betty," she added. "Tell us what else he has to say."

"That's pretty nearly all," said Betty truthfully. "He said he would save all the news until he saw me—us. One thing he did say," she added, dimpling: "The boys are simply wild with jealousy. They say it is all a deep dark scheme on Allen's part to get out here with us."

"Us!" repeated Grace, with a giggle. "Much he cares about the rest of us."

Be that as it may, they certainly all turned out that following afternoon to meet the Western Limited which was bearing Allen swiftly toward them.

There was the usual gathering of picturesquely garbed miners and cow-punchers on the platform, and for most of these the girls had a smile and a nod.

"Seems funny to think how strange everything looked to us when we first came," remarked Grace, as they waited for the train. "Now we feel as much at home as if we had lived here all our lives."

"The people are all so nice and friendly, too," said Amy. "It's wonderful how soon you come to know them."

"It is a nice atmosphere," Betty agreed. "At home in the East we want to know pretty much all there is to know about people we make our friends. But out here they take you for granted. Nobody seems to care where you came from or who your relatives are——"

"Huh," grunted Mollie. "I guess in a good many cases it wouldn't do to be too curious," she said cynically. "If you believe the stories you read and the movies you see everybody who has committed a crime anywhere from petty larceny to murder skips out West to escape just punishment."

"Then at this moment," drawled Grace, glancing around at the rather harmless looking crowd on the station platform, "we are surrounded by thieves and murderers. Though I must say they are a pretty nice looking set," she added, and the girls giggled.

"Grace could forgive a man anything, if he was only good-looking enough," remarked Amy.

"Here comes the train!" cried Betty suddenly, as the Western Limited thundered around a curve in the distance and steamed toward them. Immediately she forgot everything but that Allen was on that train and that in a moment more she would see him——

Then Allen himself, handsome as ever, eagerly scanning the faces on the platform as he jumped from the train the instant the porter opened the door.

It took him barely a moment to discover the group of girls, and he came toward them, hand outstretched, eyes alight with greeting.

"Well, if this isn't great!" he cried in his hearty voice, shaking hands with all of them but looking mostly at Betty. "Knew I could trust the Outdoor Girls to turn out for a rousing welcome. How's everything?"

"Just fine," they assured him, and then Betty took him in hand.

"We've brought a wagon along from the ranch to carry your luggage," she said, dragging him over to the wagon beside which two of the boys from the ranch were waiting bashfully. "Come over and meet a couple of our cow-punchers, and they will help you load your trunk on board."

All this accomplished, the cowboys and Allen having formed an immediate and staunch friendship, Betty introduced the latter to the horse she had brought for him to ride. The pony was a magnificent animal, dark brown in color with a curve to his graceful neck and a flash to his eye that proclaimed his thoroughbred ancestry.

"Say, you old peach of a horse," said Allen, fondly stroking the soft muzzle, "you're just about the most perfect thing of your kind I've ever seen. It seems almost a sacrilege to ride you."

"His name is Lightning," Amy volunteered. "The boys call him that because he can outrun almost any other horse on the ranch. Though," she added loyally, "I shouldn't wonder if Lady could beat him if they should give her a head start."

This characteristic speech brought a laugh, and Allen regarded the four other beautiful horses in the group.

"You girls seemed to have picked winners yourselves," he said admiringly. He studied them a moment, then his eyes narrowed quizzically as he turned to Betty.

"I'll bet you a box of candy against a pair of gloves," he said, "that I can tell which horse belongs to which. Do you take me?"

"Of course," said Betty. "Go ahead."

He guessed them nearly right, except that he gave Nigger to Mollie and Old Nick to Betty.

"Almost does not avail," sang Betty gayly. "You owe me a box of candy, Allen Washburn."

He looked at her for a moment laughing, and suddenly her gaze faltered. There had been something new and forceful about Allen ever since he had come back from the war that had made Betty a little afraid of him. But she did not think any the less of him—oh, no indeed!

"I'll give you a dozen of them if you'll take them," he was saying ardently—evidently in reference to the candies.

"And if she won't take 'em, I will," said Grace, with a gusto that made them all laugh.

On the way home the girls, with what they thought was great consideration, cantered along in front, leaving Allen and Betty to bring up the rear. Allen blessed them for it, but Betty was furious and kept up such a running fire of comment and laughing narrative that Allen had no chance to say the things he had wanted to say.

Only once as they neared the ranch she paused a moment, pointing out over the dazzling plains to the purple tipped mountains in the distance.

"Isn't the country beautiful, Allen?" she asked breathlessly. "I've fallen dead in love with it."

"It looks too good to be true," Allen agreed seriously, then added boyishly, with a glance that took her in, as well as the scenery: "Just now, I don't care if I never go home!"

CHAPTER XVI

A TIP

For the next few days the girls took possession of Allen, showing him the sights with a will and showering him with details of their adventures till the poor fellow's head was in a whirl and he could hardly tell whether it was the wolves or the landslide that had frightened the girls into the cave on that memorable afternoon.

"Seems to me," he said, as the girls showed him the cave—at a safe distance from the mountain, one may be sure—"that you young ladies need a chaperone pretty badly."

"Do you think you're it?" teased Mollie.

"Great guns! I should hope not," said Allen, with a flash of his white teeth. "I would rather face a dugout full of Boches than try to keep tabs on you girls. See here," he added, suddenly serious. "Do you mean to tell me that you were really caught in that cave with your horses and nothing to dig your way out with but your hands?"

"And a few sharp stones that we found," Betty nodded soberly.

Allen whistled softly.

"No, I should think not," he said slowly. "It's a wonder that with you and your horses, too, in that small space, you didn't smother before aid could reach you."

"We should have," spoke up Amy quickly, "if it hadn't been for Betty. She was the one who kept us at it when we were ready to give up."

"Yes, and she was the one that kept at it when the rest of us *had* given up," Mollie reminded her. "She was the one who kept digging until she forced the hole through. If it hadn't been for her we would have all given up and just died there, I guess."

Betty, who had been getting redder and redder through this recital of her heroism, found it hard to meet Allen's eyes as he turned to her with all his heart in his own.

"The girls give me altogether too much credit," she protested. "Anybody will fight when he has his back against the wall. And now let's take Allen to see Dan Higgins' mine," she added lightly. "Dan Higgins and his daughter Meggy are great friends of ours, Allen, and I know you will love them as much as we do."

"Your friends will always be mine," Allen assured her gallantly, and they rode off gayly toward Gold Run.

On the way they told him a good deal of Dan Higgins and Meggy, and Allen listened with sympathetic interest.

"That surely is tough," he said boyishly. "But of course his case is no different from that of hundreds of others who have come out here to 'God's Country' in the hope of beating the daily grind and jumping to fortune at one fell swoop. That sounds rather Irish, doesn't it?" he added, with his contagious grin.

"You're right about that, I suppose," said Betty gravely. "As you say, Dan Higgins is just one of a hundred others in the same pitiful fix. But at least he has had his dreams and the excitement of gambling. He chose this sort of life, and so we don't feel so awfully sorry for him. But it is his daughter Meggy that we pity. She is really a wonderful girl, Allen, and to condemn her to a life of work and poverty is really a crime."

"Well, I didn't do it," said Allen plaintively, adding quickly as Betty's face clouded: "I beg your pardon, little girl, I didn't mean to be flippant. But, like her father, there are many others in the position of this girl. A man can't choose to live a life like that without dragging his family into it too."

"Then he shouldn't have a family," said Mollie hotly. "He should make up his mind to be an old bachelor—though I don't think there is anything worse under the sun," she added, with such emphasis that the girls giggled.

"I agree with you there," said Allen, adding whimsically: "But what a man should do and what he does do are often very different things."

"But you speak of Dan Higgins and Meggy as if they were just ordinary people," Grace objected, as she flicked the reins gently on Nabob's arching neck. "You seem to forget that they saved our lives—probably."

"No, I don't forget that," said Allen gravely. "And I respect your wish to do something in return. I also owe them a debt of gratitude." His eyes unconsciously sought Betty's, and a quick glance passed between them that was more eloquent than words.

"Then you will help us to help him?" said Betty quickly.

"I'll do anything I can," Allen answered, adding, rather dubiously: "But I don't see what any one can do for them. If the old man hasn't struck gold yet and is short of funds to finance further search, I don't see what any one can do for him. Do you?" he added, looking at her.

"No-o," admitted Betty reluctantly. "I haven't thought of a way yet. But I'm sure I shall," she added so bravely that the girls wanted to hug her.

They reached the Higgins' mine soon after this, and at the sound of their approach Meggy ran eagerly out to them, as she always did. But when she saw Allen, looking to her unsophisticated eyes like some hero out of a story book, handsome and city-bred, she halted and turned red with embarrassment.

However, Allen, by his own gracious and friendly manner, soon set her at ease, but her eyes continued to follow every movement of his as though in amazement that such a perfect creature could live.

"Better look out, Betty," Grace whispered to the Little Captain when nobody was looking. "Meggy thinks Allen is pretty nice. Just watch her, she's hypnotized."

But Betty only smiled. Somehow, she felt pretty sure of Allen.

The latter struck up a great friendship with old Dan Higgins right away—wonderful how everybody took to Allen, thought Betty proudly—and soon they were talking like old friends. In five minutes Allen had found out more about Dan Higgins' mine and his prospects than the girls would have learned in a year.

Toward the end Allen managed to put a few adroit questions concerning Gold Run Ranch and the possibility of there being gold upon it.

"Waal now," drawled Higgins, spitting upon the ground reflectively, "folks here'bouts used to wonder why old Jed Barcolm didn't get busy and find out if there was gold on thet property, but somehow th' old man never seemed to get interested. Conservative old fellow, Jed Barcolm, anyways—allus said he'd made enough raisin' cattle and didn't aim to do no prospectin' at his time o' life."

"But you think there is a good possibility of there being gold on the ranch?" insisted Allen, and the girls held their breath.

Dan Higgins gave him a shrewd look and spat once more.

"You thinkin' of doin' a little prospectin' on your own hook, Son?" he inquired.

"Heavens, no!" answered Allen with convincing sincerity, adding with a smile: "It is barely possible that my client might, though."

The old man started and stood upright, squaring his thin shoulders belligerently.

"You don't mean to tell me you're one o' those ornery lawyer cusses," he said, with a disgusted emphasis that angered the girls but apparently left Allen unmoved.

"A lawyer—but not ornery, I hope," he said pleasantly. "And my client is Mrs. Nelson, the new owner of the ranch. Is there anything else you would like to know about me?"

But the old man's anger had departed and he regarded Allen with a shrewd twinkle in his kindly blue eyes.

"Sorry, Son," he said. "I reckon there are some honest lawyers, though I never ain't met one yet—not round here leastways."

"Thanks for a rather doubtful compliment," laughed Allen. It was evident that he was enjoying the old man extremely. "I assure you, though I am not always honest, there are times when I try very hard to be." Then he suddenly added: "By the way, do you happen to know a man around here—one of those ornery lawyers—by the name of Peter Levine?"

Again Dan Higgins spat disgustedly.

"Know him!" he answered with a wealth of scorn in his voice. "I reckon most everybody round here knows him—an' they's mighty few knows any good o' him. Take my advice, Son, an' keep away from him."

"Thanks," said Allen dryly. "But the problem seems to be to keep him away from us. He is representing a client who wants to buy Gold Run Ranch."

The old man started and a gleam of excitement shot into his eyes while Meggy, seeming to share his emotion, crept closer to him.

"Peter Levine wants you to sell," he repeated eagerly, then relaxed once more into his drawl, though his eyes reflected a strange inward turmoil. "Listen, Son," he said. "Ef you let that snake in the grass argy you into sellin', you're a bigger fool 'n I take you to be. An' what's more," his voice lowered and the girls leaned forward eagerly, "if Peter wants that there property of yourn there's gold on it, you can bet your last dollar onto it. Pete ain't no angel, an' he don't work for nothing."

Burning with excitement themselves, the girls marveled that Allen could take this statement so calmly.

"Thanks for the tip," he said, in his ordinary voice. "I had some such idea myself, but it certainly helps to have my judgment backed by somebody who knows the people in the case."

CHAPTER XVII

THE NET TIGHTENS

Allen learned much about Peter Levine and his associates and about Gold Run itself in the following conversation, and when he and the girls finally said good-by to the old man and his daughter and started off down the trail again, he was more than satisfied.

As for the girls, they could hardly wait to get out of earshot of the mine before letting loose a flood of excited comment.

"Well, I don't see anything to get so excited about," said Allen, after they had rattled on for several minutes. "Dan Higgins didn't tell us anything we didn't already know— or suspect, anyway. He simply confirmed our suspicions, that's all."

"Seems to me that's enough," retorted Mollie. "It's one thing to think a thing yourself and an entirely different thing to find out somebody else thinks it too."

"Don't be an old granddaddy, Allen," Betty said, adding threateningly: "If you don't look out we won't let you have any of that wonderful gold we are going to find—not one little tiny nugget."

"That's gratitude for you," said Allen reproachfully. "Not one little nugget for a fellow who finds her a fortune."

"You haven't found it yet," Amy reminded him.

"No," said Allen suddenly animated, "I haven't found it—not yet—but I'm pretty sure I'm on the right track. Look here," he appealed to them: "It seems reasonable to me to suppose that if Peter Levine and the people above him are so anxious to get the property they know pretty well where they stand. They don't want the ranch simply because they *think* there is gold on it."

"Then you think——" Betty was beginning breathlessly, when Allen interrupted her with a rush of words.

"Yes, that's just what I think," he said. "I've been pretty well over the whole of this ranch since I came, and I've noticed that this extreme northwest portion of it, the only part where there would be any possibility of finding gold, is pretty well deserted most of the time—absolutely so at night——"

"Then you think," Betty burst forth, "that these people, whoever they are, may have made actual tests? That they are sure there is gold here?"

Allen nodded.

"That is my theory," he said gravely. "But of course the only way to prove the truth of it is to keep my eyes open and catch them, if that is possible, in the act."

"But how could one conceal such a thing?" Grace objected. "A big thing like a mine can't be hidden away in the daytime like a rag doll. There must be some signs about the place to show that people have been here——"

"Exactly," said Allen. "There probably are signs—only nobody has had the incentive—or the interest, maybe—to hunt for those signs up to this time. Although," he added thoughtfully, "there are many ways of camouflaging the entrance to a mine so that a casual observer, even an interested one, possibly, would be fooled—branches, leaves, a rock or two."

"But wouldn't there be noise?" It was Amy who put the objection this time. "I should think they would make enough disturbance to rouse suspicion at least."

"They might not," Allen contended. "Remember, they are right in the mining territory, so that if any of the miners heard an unusual noise they would think it was one of their neighbors working late. Anyway," he finished, "their operations would necessarily have to be small, and they might be so small as not even to arouse suspicion. Sometimes," he added, and the girls hung on his words as though they were prophetic, "there need be no actual digging to ascertain that there is gold in a certain region. Sometimes the bed of a spring if sifted to get rid of pebbles and other débris will reveal gold enough to make the finder certain that there is a rich gold vein close by."

"Goodness, let's go and hunt up some springs!" cried Mollie irrepressibly. "What's the use of leaving all this gold finding to Mr. Peter Levine?"

"I remember seeing an old broken sieve around the ranch house somewhere," Grace suggested helpfully. "Don't you suppose we can go back and get it?"

"But, Allen," Betty asked anxiously, "how do you expect to find out about these men? I suppose you intend to show them up?"

"I most certainly do," responded Allen cheerfully. "It would give me the greatest delight to land Mr. Peter Levine and his associates in jail."

"Well, you'd better look out you don't get landed yourself," said Mollie sagely. "I imagine these particular gentlemen are pretty handy with their guns—like most of the other people around here—and I reckon they wouldn't be very backward about using them."

"It would be fifty-fifty, at that," said Allen, adding grimly: "I'm not so very unhandy with a gun myself. But the war's over and I haven't any idea of staging a tragedy," he added lightly, anxious to banish the cloud that had come over Betty's bright face. "I shall keep out of sight till I have them just where I want them, and when they find themselves caught I don't think they'll do much fighting. All crooks are more or less cowards, you know."

"But what are you going to do in the meantime—while you are waiting for a chance to show them up?" Betty persisted. She did not half like the way things were going—even if there was a chance of finding a fortune on the ranch. It seemed to her that Allen was putting himself into too great danger. And if anything happened to him, what would all the gold in the world be worth?

"'In the meantime?'" Allen was answering her question lightly. "Why, in the meantime I intend to keep my eyes and ears wide open and do a little scouting around Gold Run until I get a line on the doings of Peter Levine and his crowd—if he has a crowd. He may just be in partnership with one other rascal like himself, for all I know. That's one of the first things I want to find out. After the information of our friend, back there at the mine," he added, "there is no longer any doubt in my mind that this Levine is a crook."

"Humph," said Betty, "I was sure of that the first time I laid eyes on him."

"And yet you said you could almost love him for making your mother decide to come out here," Allen reminded her quizzically.

"And you said you were on your way to kill him," said Betty, adding with a chuckle: "What made you change your mind?"

"I didn't change my mind," retorted Allen, with a grin. "I just didn't happen to meet him, that's all."

They had nearly reached the ranch house before Betty thought to ask Allen if he had talked his plans over with her mother.

"No, I haven't," he admitted. "As a matter of fact, I hadn't made any definite plans until I had this confab with Dan Higgins. He made me see the whole thing straight, so to speak. I'll have a talk with your mother and father to-night," he promised.

He kept his promise and had the satisfaction of knowing that both his clients were backing him heartily.

"Go to it, Allen," Mr. Nelson said at the end of the conference. "Seems to me that you have gotten the correct angle on this thing, and if you need any help from me just call on me. Only," he warned, "don't run yourself into unnecessary trouble."

"I've found, sir," said Allen, with that straight-forward look that made every one like and admire him, "that it's usually the fellow who runs away from trouble who gets the most of it. I'm not worrying about that end of the business."

But if he did not worry, Betty certainly did in the days that followed. She had dreams at night in which she saw Allen riding about in the shadows. There would be a report, two reports, and he would topple over backwards to lie crumpled up and motionless. No wonder that she became pale and lost her appetite and made her mother worry even in the midst of the excitement over this double hunt—the hunt for men and gold.

One night after dinner Allen asked her to ride with him a little way, said it would do him a lot of good just to talk to her. Betty agreed, and they cantered off in the twilight, their bodies swaying to the rhythm of the beautiful animals under them.

For a long time they were silent, just enjoying the rapid motion, the sweet scented air that fanned their faces, the beauty of the hazy mountains in the distance. Then, suddenly Allen spoke.

"Betty," he said, swinging round toward her, "you aren't letting this thing get on your nerves, are you?"

"Wh-what do you mean?" she asked faintly. "What thing?"

"This gold business—the excitement of it all," he said, waving his hand largely as though to take in the whole landscape. "I've noticed you looked tired lately," he went on gently, "and I've worried about it, little Betty. I—I have almost dared to hope," he leaned toward her, but Betty was looking the other way, "that you were a little anxious about me. Were you?"

"Why—I—yes—no—why—I don't know," cried Betty wildly, then, meeting his eye, she laughed, a twinkling little laugh. "You shouldn't ask questions like that, not so suddenly, anyway," she said primly. "It isn't fair."

"Never mind, I got my answer," said Allen jubilantly, and again Betty found it a little hard to look at him. "You mustn't worry though, little girl," he went on gently. "There isn't any danger—really. I'm just playing a delightful little game—and I'm going to win. Went to see Levine to-day, representing your mother," he added, and his tone suddenly became grim. "He made me feel, or at least he tried to make me feel, that he had as much respect for my ability as he would for a little speck of dirt."

"The very idea!" cried Betty indignantly. "I'd just like to tell him what I think of—your ability——" she faltered on these last words, for Allen was gazing at her with a most disconcerting light in his eyes.

Suddenly she whirled Nigger's head about and urged him to a gallop.

"Race you home, Allen!" she challenged. "Winner gets the other fellow's piece of cake."

140

"Who cares for cake!" cried Allen, but it might have been noticed that he followed her just the same.

CHAPTER XVIII

IN THE SHADOWS

Allen was acting in two capacities at this time—that of lawyer and that of private detective. He probably would not have taken this rôle for anybody but Betty and her family, but in order to serve them he was willing to do pretty nearly anything.

So he had taken to scouting around the northern end of the ranch after dark, in the hope that he might possibly discover something that would help him in his theory that there was really gold on the ranch and, also, that Peter Levine and his cronies, whoever they were, knew of it.

However, as the days passed, bringing no new developments, the young fellow began to think that he had let his imagination run away with him. He even began to formulate plans by which he could lure the unsuspecting Peter Levine into telling what he knew.

And then—just when he was beginning to despair of being any help at all to Betty and her family—fate or luck, or whatever one wishes to call it, chose to smile upon him once more.

He was prowling around when quite unexpectedly he found himself confronted by Andy Rawlinson. He had struck up quite a liking for the head cowboy, and the two walked along together.

Gradually they neared a patch of timber near the northern boundary of the ranch. The cowboy said he was looking for two calves that had strayed away.

"And it ain't no use to follow 'em into the woods on hossback," he explained.

"I have an object in coming here," declared Allen, at last. "I am watching out for Peter Levine." He felt he could trust Rawlinson.

"I thought as much," replied the head cowboy, with a chuckle. "Believe me, I wouldn't trust Levine out o' my sight, if I was the boss. I've seen him prowlin' around here several times."

"Then you think he has some secret motive in getting hold of the ranch?"

"Sure as shootin'. That feller is a bad one—take it from me."

"Please don't make too much noise around here," went on Allen. "I was thinking he might come again in the dark some night—to do a little prospecting, or something like that."

"I get you. It would be just like him. Quiet it is." And after that the pair spoke only in whispers.

Nothing was seen of the calves, and presently Rawlinson was on the point of going back, when, all at once, something occurred to make him remain.

The night was intensely dark; not a star twinkled through the storm clouds that scudded across the sky. Allen had just stubbed his toe on a projecting root and had muttered something uncomplimentary to the darkness of the night when an unusual sound caught the ears of the two young men and stopped them dead in their tracks.

Some one was coming through the brush. Some one, like Allen, had stumbled and was muttering under his breath.

"Shut up, can't you?" a second voice growled, and Allen's hand instinctively went to Rawlinson's arm to quiet him.

"Two of them," he thought exultantly, as he held himself and the cowboy against the trunk of a tree. "There may be some action after all."

The two strangers passed close enough to Allen and Rawlinson to have touched them. But they did not notice the young men.

Allen and the cowboy, their blood tingling with excitement, followed the pair, and when, some hundred yards on, the strangers stopped, they stopped too, keeping within the shadow of the trees.

The strangers were bending over some sort of paper which they were examining by the light of an electric torch.

"Here's the place, Jim," one of the men said, pointing first to the paper and then into the shadow of the woods. "There's gold running wild around here, man. I've tested the bed of the creek that runs down there, and it's chock full of yellow men. Why, if we can get hold of this ranch we're rich men—rich over night, I tell you!"

"Huh!" grunted the other, noncommittally. "How are you goin' to get hold of this ranch? Ain't done it yet, so's any one could notice it."

"No, that's where you come in, Jim," replied the other, and as he turned eagerly to his companion Allen and Rawlinson recognized the features of Peter Levine. "This woman, this Mrs. Nelson who owns the place, won't sell. I'm afraid she may have an idea that there's gold here. And she suspects me, for some reason."

The other man laughed unpleasantly.

"'Tain't hard for most of us to guess the reason for that, Pete." And at the sneer Levine gave a grunt.

"You must have your little joke, Jim," he said. "But now let's get down to business. The woman distrusts me and she has sent for this insolent cub lawyer—Washburn, his name is. He's been to see me already, the unwhipped pup," he went on, while in the shadows Allen's hands gripped themselves into fists, "trying to find out more about my client and John Josephs. Say, that's a good joke, Jim. Here they are after that imaginary ranchman, John Josephs, and my client who they think are crooks, when all the time little Peter Levine is their meat and they don't know it."

"You didn't let on you wuz the one that wanted the place?" questioned Jim, who was evidently able to appreciate this joke. "You wuz just the lawyer, and so nowise interested except jest in the fee?"

"Righto!" chuckled the other. "And a good-sized fee it will be if once I can get my hands on it."

"Which you ain't—yet," the other reminded him. "Get busy, Pete, and tell us your scheme. I don't want to be standin' around here all night." He gave an uneasy glance over his shoulder, and Allen and Rawlinson shrank still further into the shadows. They were not yet ready to make their presence known.

"All right," said Peter Levine, speaking hurriedly. "If you'll agree to my suggestion, you're in for easy money, Jim. All you have to do is to approach this Mrs. Nelson and make her an offer for the ranch—for yourself, you understand. She doesn't know you, and she may have become tired of mooning around here by now, and there's just a chance that she'll take you—that is, if you handle the cards right. No eagerness, you understand—just sort of offhand and careless, as if you didn't care much whether she took you or not."

"Huh!" said the other, with his noncommittal grunt. "Sounds easy, don't it? But what do I get out of it, ef I pull this deal off, eh?"

"Half of all the gold we find, Jim," said the other, waving his hand largely. "You'll never regret it if you put this thing through. You'll be a rich man."

"All right, I'm on," said Jim.

"Then I guess it's about time we got back," returned Peter Levine, and the two men moved as if to leave that vicinity.

"We don't want them to get away," Allen whispered excitedly to Rawlinson. "I want to get hold of that paper if possible."

"I reckon that will be easy, Washburn," returned the head cowboy. "I'm armed, you know, and I'll take my chances against those two rascals any time. Just follow me."

Without waiting for Allen to reply to this, Andy Rawlinson ran forward swiftly and silently, and in a few seconds had confronted the rascally pair. He had drawn his pistol, but he did not raise the weapon.

"Halt, both of you!" he cried, sharply. "Hands up there!"

"Hi! what's the meaning of this?" cried Levine, in astonishment. "Who are you?"

"It's Rawlinson, the head man here," muttered the man called Jim.

"Right!" answered the cowboy. "And here is a particular friend of yours, Levine," he added, as Allen stepped closer.

"Washburn!" muttered the rascally lawyer from Gold Run. And then he added quickly: "Have you been spying on us?"

"If we have, that's our affair," answered Allen coolly. "You'd better keep those hands up," he went on quickly, as he saw the two rascals making a move as if to start something.

"They'll keep 'em up all right enough," broke in Rawlinson. "I reckon you know me," he went on sternly. "And I'll stand for no foolin'."

"We haven't been doing anything wrong," came from Levine, lamely.

"Oh, no! Of course not!" said Allen sarcastically. "Only trying to get hold of a bonanza for next to nothing!"

"Wait a minute, Washburn," came from the head cowboy. "Just relieve 'em of their weapons first. Then maybe we'll be able to talk with more satisfaction."

With Rawlinson confronting them, Levine and his companion did not dare offer any resistance, and quickly Allen took their weapons from them and handed the firearms to Rawlinson.

"Now I'll thank you, Levine, for that paper you were examining so carefully just a few minutes ago," went on the young lawyer.

"This is robbery!" fumed Peter Levine. "I'll have you before the courts for this."

Allen eyed him steadily.

"Do you represent the law in this place?" he asked. "If so, I am sorry for the inhabitants. But there is no use in prolonging this discussion, Levine. I want that paper. Hand it over at once."

The rascally lawyer from Gold Run attempted to argue, but the sight of Rawlinson's weapon subdued him, and presently he handed over the crumpled sheet, which Allen seized with muc satisfaction. During this transaction Jim remained sullenly silent.

"Now I guess that's about all," said Allen to the cowboy.

"If that's the case I guess we can bid you skunks good-evening," came quickly from Rawlinson. "Both of you beat it. And don't ever let me ketch you around here again."

"What about my gun?" came feebly from Jim.

"I'll send the guns over to Levine's office to-morrow," answered the head cowboy. "Now clear out, and be quick about it." And a moment later the two rascals stumbled away through the darkness.

"This is certainly what I call luck," cried Allen excitedly, as he gazed at the scrap of paper Levine had passed over. "Rawlinson, you have certainly helped me do a good night's work. If what that scoundrel said is true, this will mean a fortune for Betty and her mother."

"I'm glad I chanced along, Washburn," answered the head cowboy. "After this I think I'll set a guard. If it leaks out that there is gold on this ranch there will be all sorts of fellows beside those skunks trying to locate claims around here."

"Will you go up to the house with me?"

"No. I'll stick around here a while and see if those fellows come back. Besides, I want to see if I can get any trace of those strayed-away calves. You go ahead. You can tell me about it later. You can take their guns with you if you will."

Half running, half stumbling, in his eagerness, Allen reached the house, took the steps of the porch three at a time, and burst into the big homelike kitchen, where he found the family assembled.

"We've got 'em, folks!" he cried, waving the scrap of paper over his head, while they stared at him as though they thought he had gone mad. "I've been out hunting and brought home a prize. Come look at it."

He went over to the table beside which Mr. and Mrs. Nelson were sitting and laid the two captured pistols upon the table. Infected by his excitement, the girls crowded around, demanding an explanation.

THE GIRLS CROWDED AROUND, DEMANDING AN EXPLANATION.

The Outdoor Girls in the Saddle.

"Pistols!" cried Betty, her eyes wide with dislike of the things. "Where did you get them, Allen?"

"Oh, just picked them off the trees by the roadside," said Allen airily. Then, suddenly becoming serious, he laid the scrap of paper beside the weapons on the table. "There," he said, dramatically, "is the key that may open your door to a fortune."

"A map," said Mrs. Nelson, her eyes glistening. "Oh, Allen, you've found out something wonderful. Tell us about it, please."

And so Allen recounted what had taken place during that fruitful half hour in the shadows of the trees. His audience listened breathlessly.

"Then this thing," said Mr. Nelson, taking the bit of paper which was crossed and criss-crossed with a number of lines and dotted with numbers until it seemed more like a jig-saw puzzle than a map, "is supposedly a map which will point out the probable location of gold."

"Yes, sir," said Allen.

"Then," said Mr. Nelson, feeling the thrill of adventure in his own blood, "we'll begin to look for this gold to-morrow. That is—" He paused and looked quizzically about at the group of tense young faces. "If everybody is willing."

"Oh-h," was all that they could say—just then.

CHAPTER XIX

THE NEW MINE

The next day much excitement filled the ranch house. Betty declared that she had not slept a wink the night before, worrying for fear her father had not meant what he said.

But Mr. Nelson had meant what he had said, and there was Mrs. Nelson as eager as the girls to keep him to his word.

"The ranch is mine, you know," she laughingly reminded the girls. "And if there are gold mines on it I certainly intend to find them."

It was settled, and Mr. Nelson and Allen set out for town to make arrangements for the enterprise. The girls wanted to go too, but Mr. Nelson pointed out that he and Allen could probably do the work more quickly if they were alone, and it was upon this point and this point only that the girls consented to let them go.

"But that needn't keep us from the saddle," Mollie decided, as they watched the two men canter swiftly away. "I don't know about the rest of you, but I'm just longing for action."

"Ditto," cried Betty, then added with bright eagerness: "Girls, I know what we can do! Let's go down to the place where Allen found those two men last night. That's where the mines are, you know, and we might stake out claims or something."

"Your mother might have something to say to that," said Grace, making a funny face. "It isn't quite the thing to stake out claims on somebody else's property."

"Oh well, you needn't be so particular," cried Betty airily. "Come on, girls, who's with me?"

It seemed they all were, and, fairly dancing with excitement, they made their way to the corrals where Andy Rawlinson saddled their horses for them.

The horses seemed to catch some of the girls' excitement, and it was all that the latter could do to hold the animals in.

"It must be in the air," laughed Grace, as she pulled in Nabob sharply. "We've all got the gold fever."

"Let's give them their heads," said Mollie suddenly. "I'd like a regular gallop this morning."

"All right, let's go," sang out Betty, and in another minute they were off, the horses galloping like mad and the girls laughing and shouting in utter abandonment to their high spirits.

At this rate it took them only a few minutes to reach the spot where Allen had had his adventure the night before.

They reined in sharply, and Betty jumped down, throwing the reins over Nigger's neck and giving him a fond little pat on the flank.

"There, old boy," she said. "Go and eat some grass for yourself while we do a little prospecting. Girls," she added as they in turn dismounted and ran up to her, "from Allen's description, it must have been just about here that he stood." She indicated the bent tree with the great bowlder behind it that Allen had described to them. "And the two men must have stood in there among that heavy shrubbery somewhere."

"Then this is where they will begin work," cried Amy, a faint flush warming her face. "Oh, Betty, it all seems like a fairy story."

"Fairy story, nothing!" exclaimed Mollie. "This is a real, honest-to-goodness adventure story. My, it's a wonder Allen didn't get shot up last night," she added thoughtfully. "It must have taken nerve to stand here, listening to those old scoundrels and not knowing what minute they might find him out and fire upon him."

"I think Allen is perfectly wonderful, anyway," said Grace, and Betty thrilled at the tribute. "He never seems to know what it is to be afraid. And he always gets what he wants, too."

"And to think that 'John Josephs' never existed!" chuckled Betty. "Peter Levine must have quite a good deal of imagination."

"Well, what's the use of standing here?" said Amy, after a moment of silent musing. "Let's look around a little bit and see what we can see."

So for a while they thrashed around in the bush, accomplishing very little besides scaring some rabbits and woodchucks into their holes. They found the tiny creek Peter Levine had spoken of, and they gazed with interest at its muddy, sluggish water.

"Who would ever think there was gold in the bottom of that?" whispered Mollie.

When they finally became convinced that there was nothing more to be seen they started reluctantly home again.

"Let's go around by the mine and see how Meggy and her dad are coming on," suggested Betty, and so they changed their course a little to include the mine.

Meggy was glad to see them as usual but they could tell by the weariness of her bearing that there was no good news as far as she was concerned and they had not the heart to tell her their own.

"Can't you come over to the ranch for a little while?" asked Betty, eager to do some little thing toward cheering the girl. But Meggy shook her head.

"I can't leave father—even for a little while," she said sadly. "He ain't feeling well, and I'm afraid if his luck doesn't change pretty soon I—I—won't have any dad——" she choked and turned away. Betty was beside her in a moment, her arm about the girl's shoulders.

"We're awfully sorry, honey," she said compassionately. "We didn't know that your father was feeling bad. Is he—is he really sick?"

"Sick of life, I guess," said Meggy, conquering her emotion and instantly ashamed of it. "I've heered of people dyin' of a broken heart, an' that's what dad's doin', I guess. Bad luck can kill you if it keeps up long enough."

The girls rode home saddened by this brief encounter. It seemed almost wrong for them to be happy when Dan Higgins was "dyin' of a broken heart" and Meggy, brave, splendid girl that she was, had almost lost hope.

"If only everybody in the world could be happy," said Grace plaintively. "It just spoils all your fun when you know that other people are miserable."

"The worst of it is," said Betty soberly, "that with all this luck coming our way we can't pass on a single little bit of it to that poor girl and her dad. If only they weren't so proud——" The sentence trailed off into a sigh, and she gazed pensively out over the plain.

"Well, there's no use of crying over it," said Mollie briskly. "We may find a way of being useful to Meggy yet, and until then, as my mother says, 'let's be canty with thinking about it.' Oh, look, girls, here comes Allen. I wonder what kind of news he has."

They galloped gayly to meet him, and Allen thought they made a very pretty picture as they swept up to him.

"Well," he said as they surrounded him, "everything is settled and they are to begin work to-morrow morning. Our news has aroused great excitement in town, and there's a rush to establish claims near that end of our ranch. Better give your friend, Dan Higgins, a hint, so that he can get in first. So long. I'm on to the house for the map, and then I'm going to join Mr. Nelson again in town."

So he dashed off in the direction of the ranch and the girls wheeled and galloped back in the direction they had come—back toward Dan Higgins' mine to warn him to stake a new claim before others reached the spot.

They were so excited that it was hard to make their purpose clear at first, but when the old man and Meggy comprehended what they were trying to tell them, they were immediately galvanized to action.

"I'll show you the best place," Betty eagerly volunteered.

Mollie offered to stay behind and give the old man her horse, and in a minute Betty and Dan Higgins were galloping over the plain to that part of the ranch where the new gold mines were to be. They had not far to go, and they saw with relief that they were the first on the spot.

Betty pointed out the place where Peter Levine had said there was gold running wild, and old Dan Higgins staked his claim as near to the place as he could without actually encroaching upon the ranch itself.

With trembling fingers he printed on two big placards the exact dimensions of his claim, and, with Betty's help, nailed them to two trees at the two extreme ends of his new property, and began to dig.

"Thar," he sighed, after a few moments, taking off his hat to mop the perspiration from his forehead, "I've made another bargain with luck, an' mebbe this time I'll win."

"I'm sure you will," cried Betty, with conviction. "If there is gold on our ranch, and we are sure there is, then there is almost certain to be some on your property also. Oh, Mr. Dan Higgins, I so dearly hope that there is!" This was so evidently a cry straight from her earnest young heart that the keen eyes of the hardened old miner filled with tears and he patted Betty's head with an unsteady hand.

"You're a mighty fine little gal," he said finally. "Ef an old man's gratitude means anything to you, you sure have got it. I've a sort of sure feelin' you've changed the luck for Meggy and me."

They were silent on the ride back to the mine, but as they reached the last stretch of the trail that led down to it the old man shifted in his saddle and looked at Betty earnestly.

"An' ef Meggy's mother was alive," he said simply, "she would thank you, too."

CHAPTER XX

THE VIOLINIST AGAIN

As Allen had predicted, there was a general rush on the part of the miners to establish claims on the property adjoining the ranch, and the girls congratulated themselves over and over again that they had reached Dan Higgins with the glad tidings in time for him to secure the best location.

All day long the girls were in the saddle, hovering about the new gold diggings, fascinated at the way new mines seemed to spring up over night.

Next to those on their own property, they were most interested in Dan Higgins' mine and in their hearts they would really rather have had him find gold than to find it themselves.

"They need it so much more than we do," Betty said anxiously. "If Dan Higgins and Meggy have drawn another blank I don't know what they will do."

In the midst of all this confusion and excitement, Amy received the program of the benefit concert given at the Hostess House for which she had sent home some time before. They had almost forgotten the hermit and it was with a shock of surprise that they remembered they had not seen him since the new mining operations. Before that they had run across him quite often attempting to help Meggy and Dan in his rather eccentric way.

"Guess he must have been scared off by the crowd," said Mollie. "Too much excitement for the old boy."

The four of them were sitting on the large front porch of the house, still in their riding habits, while their horses, at the foot of the steps, stamped their impatience to be off again. Nothing but the arrival of the mail could have drawn the girls from the fascination of the new gold diggings. They hardly took time to eat; and as for sleep, well, they took that in between times!

Now Grace called to Amy, making room on the step beside her.

"Come over here and show us your program," she said, extracting a bit of candy from some hidden recess somewhere about her person and popping it into her mouth. "I'm anxious to see what that violinist's name was.

Amy obeyed, and as Grace opened the program. Mollie and Betty drew closer and peeped over her shoulder.

"Concerto—Liszt," read Grace, her finger pointing down the page. "No, that isn't it. That's for the piano. Hold on, here we are. Chopin—Nocturne—Paul Loup, violinist. There he is. Now will you please tell me how that helps us to find out anything about the hermit?" She paused with her finger still pointing to the name and looked up at them inquiringly.

"We-el," said Betty thoughtfully, "it doesn't help very much, I must admit. It doesn't prove that Paul Loup is our Hermit of Gold Run. Only that funny feeling I have of having seen him before and heard him play——"

"I tell you what we'll do!" Mollie snapped her fingers decisively. "It's a long chance and it may not work at all but—are you game to try it?" She paused and regarded the expectant girls eagerly.

"Maybe," said Betty, noncommittally. "You might tell us the idea first."

"Listen," cried Mollie. "My idea is that if we take the hermit by surprise, call him by his name of Paul Loup. Why—" She paused, and the light of inspiration filled her eyes. "I could even speak to him in French——"

As the girls caught her full meaning they looked at her admiringly.

"I shouldn't wonder if that plan would work," said Betty swiftly. "Why can't we go now? Dinner won't be ready for a couple of hours."

"Right you are," cried Mollie, taking the four steps at one jump and springing upon her astonished horse. "Come on, girls, are you with us?"

"We'll have to lead 'em a merry pace," said Betty to Mollie a moment later as they galloped abreast up the road. "If we don't get them there in a hurry they're apt to get cold feet and think we're crazy."

"Maybe we are," chuckled Mollie, urging Old Nick on to even greater speed. "I've had a suspicion that way several times before."

It was Betty's turn to chuckle.

"So have I!" she said, adding with a sigh of resignation: "But oh, it is so much fun. Look behind, Mollie. Are they still coming?"

"Strong," reported Mollie, with a glance over her shoulder. Then, as they reached the trail that led through the woods, she reined in a little, motioning for Betty to take the lead. "You know the trail better," she said.

Over the rough woodland trail their progress necessarily became slower, a fact which the girls did not relish at all. It gave them time to reflect on what a really rash adventure they had embarked, and any but the Outdoor Girls might have turned back even at this last minute.

However, curiosity, together with some vague hope that they might become of service to this strange sad fellow, urged them on. If Paul Loup and the Hermit of Gold Run were really one and the same person, then surely there was a real mystery which they might in some way help to unravel.

They did not linger any longer on the way than was absolutely necessary, for the terrible experience they had had with the timber wolves soon after their arrival had made them suspicious of the forest, and try as they would they could not suppress an uncomfortable desire to search every shadow for some sinister, lurking presence.

In vain had the cowboys on the ranch assured them that wolves were very scarce in this part of the forest, especially in the summer, and that they had had an unusual and unique experience. As Amy had said, one experience like that was enough to last a lifetime.

They came in sight of the cabin without mishap, however, and they tethered their horses a little farther from the house than usual, so that their stamping and neighing might not frighten the hermit away.

Then they made their way with as little noise as possible along the narrow path.

"Suppose he isn't at home?" whispered Mollie to Betty.

"Then we're out of luck, that's all," returned Betty cheerfully.

But the hermit was at home. They could see him moving about, and as they came nearer they smelled an appetizing odor of frying bacon, as though he were cooking his dinner.

"Hope he asks us to stay to lunch," said Grace, and the girls giggled nervously.

"We'll be lucky if he doesn't slam the door in our faces," said Amy pessimistically.

It was Mollie who knocked this time—and it was no timid little rap either, but a good, hearty rat-at-tat, that brought the occupant of the cabin to the door in a hurry. He had the frying pan still clutched in his hand and on his long narrow face was such a look of dread that the girls felt sorry for him.

"Well," he said, the emotion within him making his voice sound stern and forbidding, "what is it you wish? It is not raining to-day as it was that other time." He gazed significantly up at the cloudless sky seen in little blue patches through the trees, and the girls flushed, partly from embarrassment and partly from anger. Somehow, they had not been prepared to have him take this attitude, and they resented it.

For a moment they stood miserably tongue-tied. Even their usually quick-witted Little Captain seemed suddenly to have been stricken speechless. They were just about to turn and run when Mollie saved the day for them.

Pushing forward through the group she confronted the man on the door step.

"*Vous êtes Paul Loup, n'est-ce pas, monsieur?*" she said in a clear voice, gazing up at him fearlessly.

While the girls gasped at her temerity a most astounding thing happened. The man dropped the frying pan and it clattered to the floor, its contents spilling out greasily. While they looked he seemed to crumple, shrivel, and his eyes stared at them glassily out of his white mask of a face.

"*Mon Dieu!*" he cried hoarsely, staggering back into the shack. "You have found me! But I swear to you I did not kill him. *Mon Dieu*, I could not kill my brother!"

CHAPTER XXI

A STARTLING TALE

Hardly able to believe that they were actually living this weird thing, the girls crowded into the shack after the stricken man and found that he had sunk upon a bench and covered his face with his hands.

Strangely enough, though it had been Mollie who had precipitated this thing, it was Betty who now took the lead. Softly she went over to the shrinking man and put a gentle hand on his shoulder.

"You say you did not kill your brother?" she questioned in so calm a voice that the girls marveled at her. "You are sure you did not?"

"No! no!" cried the man again raising his haggard face, deep-lined with the marks of suffering, "No—I am not sure. Can you not see? It is that that is killing me. Yet in my sane moments I know that he was dead. He lay there, so white, so still, with only that red, red stream of blood to mar his whiteness. I leaned down, I listened to his heart——" The man had evidently forgotten the presence of the girls, engulfed as he was in the horror of the incident he related. Once more he was living the tragedy, and the girls, tense, strained, horrified, lived it with him.

"I listened to his heart," the man repeated, his arms stretched out before him, his long, delicate hands gripped with a fierceness that made the knuckles go white. "There was no beating. I put my face close to his mouth to see if there was breath. But he had stopped breathing—forever!

"My heart went cold. I seized him by the shoulders. I called him by his name—that brother that I had loved! Oh, how I had loved him. I begged him to come back to me, to open those gray lips that a moment before had been beautiful with life—to speak to me—and all the time——" his hand relaxed and pointed to the floor and the girls followed the movement fascinated—"there kept spreading and spreading on the rug a deep red stain—my brother's blood! *Mon Dieu! And when I staggered to my feet I found that the horrible stuff had clung to my fingers—they were dark and sticky—the fingers of a murderer! I went mad then, I think. I rushed from the house, from the place. One thing only was in my mind. To get away—to get away from Paris, that accursed city——" He paused, staring at the floor, and the girls waited, hardly daring to move for fear they would break the spell.

"The rest is like a bad dream to me," the man continued in a weary voice. "Ghost-ridden, haunted, I came to this country incognito—under what you call an assumed name. For a short time I stayed in New Orleans——"

"But your violin!" Betty interrupted in a voice that amazed her, it seemed so little and weak. "Surely you were under contract."

The man turned on her what was almost a pitying look from his sunken eyes.

"I could not play," he said, with a shrug of his shoulders. "To have gone to my manager would have been like going to the hangman—the electric chair, what you have in this country. No, mademoiselle, I was a murderer, a man hunted by his fellowmen.

There was but one thing for me to do—to hide, to dodge about like a rabbit from a pack of baying dogs. Hide!" he added bitterly. "I could not hide from myself.

"Always when the night grows dark and the wind it makes to howl around this place I can hear my brother's voice uplifted in anger. We quarreled over something my uncle had said—a foolish quarrel. He called me liar, and I—something snapped in my brain, I think, and for a moment everything went red. There was a wine bottle on the table—we had been drinking—blindly I struck out with it—— Now, when the darkness comes and the wildcat calls into the night with a scream like a soul in torment, I hear again the tinkling of that bottle as it shattered, the short groan, the falling of a heavy body.

"It is a wonder that I have not gone mad," he said. "Many a time I have prayed that I might or that I might find courage to end this miserable life and go to join my brother. But I am a coward, a coward——" His voice lowered till it was almost inaudible and tears trickled through the long white fingers. "I have not the courage even to die. There is a tribunal above that I should have to face, more just, more awful, than any man-made law. There you have what Paul Loup has become."

"But you must not speak that way," said Betty, whose quick mind had been forging ahead while the man had been speaking. "It is one thing to kill a man deliberately, and quite another to kill in hot blood, blindly. Besides," she added eagerly, "you are not even sure that you did kill your brother. Did you—have you seen the papers since—since you ran away?"

"No," said the man. His tone was dead, hopeless. "I was afraid of what I might find there. He was dead, Mademoiselle," he added wearily. "When I say that there is a doubt of that it is simply to give myself one little excuse for continuing to live. He did not move, he did not breathe. Ah, yes, he was dead, quite dead."

There was silence for a moment while Betty thought rapidly. Amy and Mollie and Grace stared wide-eyed with the feeling that they were witnessing some tremendous, swift-moving drama.

"Of course," said the man, breaking the silence abruptly, his somber eyes upon Betty, "there is but one thing left for me now to do. I shall surrender to the authorities—a thing which I should have done long ago. Or," he added grimly, "you might rather go with me now. If you left me I might attempt to escape—so you will think, Mademoiselle?"

There was a lift at the end of the sentence that made it a question and, startled, the girls looked at Betty to see what she would say.

The Little Captain herself was startled. Evidently the man thought they had been tracking him, had used their knowledge to trap him.

"Oh, it isn't as you think!" she cried impulsively. "We never had the slightest little wish to harm you. And please, please," she added earnestly, "don't give yourself up to the authorities, or do anything rash until you hear from me again. You may not believe me—I wouldn't blame you if you didn't——" she went on shyly, for the man had risen and was staring at her, "but all we want to do is to help you if we can——" she broke off confusedly for the look in the man's eyes silenced her.

"You know I am Paul Loup," he cried hoarsely. "You have heard my story, my confession from my own lips, and still you say that you wish me no harm! Who are you? What are you? What do you want of me?" He had advanced toward them, and in a panic the girls moved back toward the open door. Only Betty stood fearlessly in his path.

"We are the Outdoor Girls, and we are living just at present on Gold Run Ranch," she said quietly. "We found out who you were because you were good enough to play for us at a benefit we gave at the Hostess House at Camp Liberty some time ago. And we came up here because we thought that you were in trouble and that we might help you. If we can't help you, I'm sorry." And with head bravely uplifted Betty turned toward the door.

She had almost reached it when he called to her.

"You are a brave girl," said Paul Loup slowly, his eyes intent on Betty's pretty face, "How do you know that I—the murderer—will not kill you also for this knowledge you have of me?"

Betty heard the frightened gasp of the girls behind her, but, strangely enough, she herself felt no fear.

"You wouldn't do that," she said, her clear gaze holding his burning one. "You could not wish harm to a friend."

"Is that what you wish me to consider you—a friend?" asked the strange man, feeling suddenly as though something warm and vital had closed about his heart.

"If you will," replied Betty, reaching out her hand. "I would like very much to be."

But Paul Loup, for all he was a murderer and an outcast, was also a Frenchman. With a quick gesture, ignoring her outstretched hand he caught her in his arms, held her there for a minute, then, releasing her, kissed her gently, first on one cheek, then on the other.

"I had forgotten there were kind hearts in the world," he murmured brokenly, turning from her. "You have restored my faith. *Au revoir*, my friend."

Someway, somehow, the girls found themselves outside that little cabin, making their way blindly down the path to where their horses were tethered. In a daze they mounted and rode off down the trail.

When they came to the open trail they found that Betty was crying, openly, unashamed. Mollie pushed a handkerchief into her hand, but the Little Captain did not seem to notice it. She stared straight ahead, her cheeks burning, the tears rolling unchecked down her face.

"Never mind, honey," said Mollie, trying to steady her voice. "It was hard for you, I know; but I would give anything I own to have made him feel that way about me. I don't care if he did commit murder. I'm for him—strong."

"To be all alone," said Betty as though Mollie had not spoken, "and so heart-hungry that a little sympathy from a stranger——" A sob choked the rest of her sentence. But a moment later she faced the girls with a light of resolve shining in her eyes.

"Girls," she said, "I don't believe Paul Loup is a murderer, and some way or other I'm going to prove it. A man like that just couldn't commit murder. I know it!"

CHAPTER XXII

THE PLAN

Certainly the girls had never expected such startling developments from Mollie's simple little ruse to find out who the mysterious Hermit of Gold Run was. In the beginning it had been something of a lark, and they never dreamed that their interest and curiosity would uncover such a tragedy.

However, they were not at all in sympathy with Betty's conviction that Paul Loup had not really killed his brother.

"I don't see how you get that way, Betty," Grace argued hotly. "We all feel as sorry for the hermit as you do, but we have his own word for it that he really killed his brother."

"He did seem to be pretty sure of it," said Amy, with a quaver in her voice. "When the wind rose last night and wailed around the house, I got all creepy thinking of him alone up in that dreary little shack, living that whole horrible thing over again."

It was the next day, and the girls were in the saddle, as usual. They had visited the new gold diggings and found everybody excited and optimistic, though no gold had been uncovered as yet. And now they were trotting slowly along the open road, their thoughts busy with the startling happenings of the day before.

"It's a wonder he doesn't go crazy," shuddered Mollie, taking up the thread where Amy had dropped it. "I know I would. What was it he said about being 'ghost-ridden?'"

"I don't believe he is ghost-ridden at all, except by his imagination," said Betty positively. "I think if he had taken the trouble to look at the newspapers before he decided that he was a hunted man he might have saved himself a lot of trouble and unhappiness."

"Goodness, how do you get that way, Betty?" Grace said irritably. "The man ought to be the best judge of whether he killed anybody or not."

"Well," said the Little Captain stubbornly, "it seems to me it would have had to be a pretty heavy bottle with a pretty strong arm behind it to kill a man with one blow. And a scalp wound bleeds horribly, you know."

The girls looked a little thoughtful, and for the first time since Betty had advanced her theory they began to think that there might possibly be something in it after all.

"That's right," said Amy, and then went on to relate an experience she had had when skylarking with Sarah Stonington.

"She had hold of that heavy rocking chair we have in the library," Amy said. "She was trying to pull it away from me, and I was hanging on to it for dear life.

"Then suddenly I let go, and Aunt Sarah—she's pretty heavy, you know—lost her balance as the chair swung forward, and fell over backward, striking her head on the sharp edge of the piano."

"Goodness, you must have been scared," commented Mollie.

"Scared!'" echoed Amy. "Why, I was struck dumb with terror. I thought I had killed her. She lay there all white and funny, and her head was bleeding dreadfully——"

"There's your scalp wound for you," Betty pointed out. "Just a little scratch will make the whole place look like a shambles."

"But what happened to your aunt Sarah, Amy," pursued Mollie interestedly. "We know she didn't die."

"Well, I should say she didn't!" said Amy roundly. "She was as good as ever in ten minutes and laughing at me for being so frightened. But we had to have the rug sent away to get the stain out," she added significantly.

"Huh," said the girls, and once more became thoughtful.

"But suppose you were right, Betty?" said Mollie, after a while. "Suppose our poor musician is torturing himself by thinking he has committed a crime that he hasn't? What could you possibly do about it?"

"I don't just know," Betty admitted truthfully.

"We might ask your father," Grace hazarded, but Betty turned on her, startled.

"That's just the thing I don't want to do!" she said hurriedly. "Dad is just the best and most easy-going father in the world, but he has a terribly stern sense of justice. I'm not sure he wouldn't think we were making ourselves—oh, what do you call it——"

"<u>Accessories</u> after the fact?" suggested Mollie, helpfully.

"That's it," said Betty. "He might argue that we were committing a crime ourselves by helping to hide a criminal——"

"Well, maybe we are, at that," said Grace, uncomfortably.

"They can put you in jail for that sort of thing, can't they?" added Amy, a suggestion which certainly did not add to the cheerfulness of the atmosphere.

"I don't care," said Betty stoutly. "I'd rather go to jail than deliver a man to a doubtful justice—especially when he may really be innocent. Anyway," she added, reasonably: "who is there to know that we went to Paul Loup's cabin the other day? I'm very sure no one saw us go in or come out, and if we keep quiet no one will have to know. That's why I didn't even want to take dad into our confidence."

"But if our musician is, as you think, innocent," Grace insisted, "then your father could do more for him than we."

"But we don't know that he is innocent. That's only my idea," said Betty. "And dad would probably think it was a very foolish one. Maybe it is, for all I know," she added dubiously.

"How about Allen?" said Grace suddenly after another rather long silence. "He would certainly sympathize with our poor hermit and, being a lawyer, he would probably be able to think up some way that we might establish the man's innocence or guilt without giving away his whereabouts. There, how's that for a brilliant idea?" she finished proudly.

175

"I had already thought of that," admitted Betty, while the girls turned amused eyes upon her. "But I was almost afraid to suggest it."

"Maybe Allen would agree with your father that we, ought to turn him over to justice," said Mollie, but Betty shook her head vigorously.

"Never! Not Allen!" she declared fervently. "He believes the other fellow innocent until he is proved guilty."

"So does the law," said Amy wisely.

"Yes, but the law has sent many an innocent man to prison nevertheless," retorted Mollie. "We don't always find justice in the courts."

"Hear, hear," cried Grace. "Get a soap box, Mollie."

"Then it is settled that we are to tell Allen, is it?" said Betty eagerly. "I'm sure he will find some way to help us."

"If we can pry him loose from the mining outfit," laughed Mollie. "He seems to have gold fever worse than any of them."

But Allen had been busy, during the intervals when he could tear himself away from the fascination of the mining operations, on some legal matters.

Mrs. Nelson, and her husband also, had feared that these numerous relatives of her great uncle, of whose existence she herself had scarcely been aware, might see fit to contest the old man's will especially when it became apparent that his property at this time was far more valuable than it had been at the time of his death.

Allen, after considerable investigation, was able to set their fears at rest upon this point, however, by asserting that the old gentleman had made only one will and that he thought it very doubtful under the circumstances that the relatives would take the case into the courts. They were not Mr. Barcolm's children and grandchildren, as Lizzie had supposed, but distant relatives whom at one time and another the old man had befriended and gathered about him, but who had later quarreled with their benefactor.

"Anyway," Mrs. Nelson decided happily, "if we really do find some gold I will give each one of them a share of it, even to the littlest."

On this particular afternoon the girls found Allen, not at the mines as they supposed they would, but at the ranch house busy with some papers.

When they besought him to come out for a ride, he hesitated at first, saying that he ought to get his work done before night. But they finally persuaded him not to let duty interfere with pleasure.

"All right," he surrendered at last. "If you will get one of the boys to saddle Lightning for me I will be with you in ten minutes."

He kept his promise, and in a short time was listening to the strangest tale he had ever heard. As he listened his face became more and more serious.

"But, girls, this thing sounds impossible!" he burst forth, finally. "Are you telling me that you, alone and unprotected, managed to inveigle this murderer into confessing his crime to you? Gee, it's—it's unbelievable! The four of you would be a great help to me in my profession," he added, with a chuckle.

"I didn't think you would take it as a joke," said Betty, reproachfully.

"It isn't a joke," returned Allen, his face grave again. "It's a mighty serious business, if you will excuse my saying so. It makes me sick when I think of the chance you took." He was speaking to all the girls, but his look of concern was for Betty.

"Oh, we don't want to think about ourselves," said the latter, impatiently. "We've done a good deal more dangerous things than that in our lives. We thought—we hoped—you might help us to prove his innocence——"

"But the man's guilty," said Allen, surprised. "We have that by his own confession——"

With a glance of despair at the others, Betty interrupted him.

"Listen to me, Allen," she said. "This is what I think——" And she went on to tell him her idea while he listened, at first with a smile of faint amusement on his lips which gradually changed to grave admiration as he realized Betty's unfailing faith in the basic goodness of human nature.

"I hope you are right, little girl," he said at last, when she had finished and was looking at him earnestly. "I'd like to believe you were right——"

"But you can't?" she finished for him, trying to stifle the disappointment in her heart.

"No, I can't," he answered truthfully. "When a man is so sure of his crime that he flees his own country, gives up money and fame to escape the law, you may be pretty sure that his crime was a real one."

"But, Allen, you don't know the man," Betty pleaded, pretty close to tears in the bitterness of her disappointment. "No one could make the kind of music he does and be truly wicked. I wish you could have met him. I think you would have tried a little harder to help him."

"I'm willing to help him, if I can," Allen answered gently, feeling that he would be almost to step into this poor musician's place if he might have Betty plead for him as she had just done for the other. "What is it you would like me to do?"

Then suddenly the great idea popped full grown into Betty's head.

"I have it!" she cried. "Why not write to Paul Loup's manager in New York and ask him for particulars?"

"Capital!" replied Allen approvingly, while the girls looked at their Little Captain admiringly. "If anybody ought to be able to give us information, he surely is the one."

"And, Allen," begged Betty, reining her horse close to Allen and laying a timid hand on his arm, "you won't even whisper a word of what we've told you—not for your foolish old law, or anything else?"

"Of course not," said Allen, smiling at her. "We have to give the poor fellow his chance."

CHAPTER XXIII

GREAT DAYS

That very afternoon Allen composed a letter to Paul Loup's concert manager—advised and censored by the girls, of course—and they all rode off to town to mail it in time to catch the four o'clock outgoing mail.

"Now," said Mollie, as, this duty well performed, they started back to the ranch, "I feel better. We've started something, anyway."

"Let's hope that we can finish it," added Grace, dubiously.

They did not expect an answer to this epistle within ten days, and in the meantime they found plenty to keep them busy around the ranch.

Progress at the mines was swift, and almost any minute now they might expect to hear the glorious tidings that some one had "struck it rich."

Nothing had been seen of Peter Levine since that memorable night when the map had been taken from him, and it was rumored that the rascally lawyer had left town.

"And the longer he keeps away the healthier it will be for him, I reckon," Allen said, adding with a laugh: "Gee, but it makes me happy every time I think of how sore that chap may be."

Betty had dimpled sympathetically.

"You have an awfully mean disposition, Allen," she chided him.

Meggy and Dan Higgins were working furiously at their mine, but after a few days Betty was quick to see that they were not progressing as well as some of the others. After all Meggy, though unusually strong and robust for her age, was only a girl and her father was an old man who had just about worn out his energies in a fruitless search for fortune.

Betty had besought her father to send help to these good friends of hers, and Mr. Nelson had immediately complied.

There had been some trouble with Dan at first—with Meggy too, for that matter.

"We can't take nothin' thet we can't pay fer, sir," the old fellow assured Mr. Nelson positively. But the latter reminded him that he and Meggy had saved his daughter's life, as well as those of the other girls, and that this put him, Mr. Nelson, deeply in the others' debt. In view of this the old fellow finally surrendered. In his heart he was deeply, fervently thankful for the help of the young, able-bodied man whom Mr. Nelson provided and for whose services he paid.

"But ef I strike thet thar gold vein, sir," Dan assured Mr. Nelson earnestly, "I'm goin' to make it up to you, sir, every cent of it."

"All right, we can talk about that later," Mr. Nelson said, and laughed and walked on to view his own operations, feeling that he had done a very good day's work.

One morning, as the girls mounted their horses and turned their heads in the direction of the gold diggings, they heard what seemed to be wild cheering and shouting in the distance and with one impulse they urged their horses to a gallop.

"Somebody's found something!" shouted Mollie, as the cheering and shouting became more distinct. "Oh, girls, I wonder who it is."

"Maybe a mine has caved in, or something," Grace called back, pessimistically. "You'd better not get too happy, all at once."

"You old wet-blanket!" cried Betty, as she leaned forward and whispered in Nigger's ear, urging him to greater speed. "That kind of mine doesn't cave in very often. Oh, Nigger, hurry, old boy! Don't you know we've got to get there quickly?"

As they approached the noise became tumultuous, and as they topped a small hill that brought them in full view of the new diggings they saw a sight that they would never forget as long as they lived.

They gazed on what seemed to be a mob gone wild. Men grasped each other around the waists, performing some kind of crazy dance that looked like an Indian cakewalk. Others tossed their hats in the air and shot holes through them as they fell to the ground. And all were laughing, crying, shouting, waving arms and head gear in a sort of wild, feverish, primal jubilation.

The girls caught the thrill of it and they tingled to their finger tips. Putting spurs to their horses, they galloped down into the thick of it.

CHAPTER XXIV

THE END OF PETER LEVINE

The crowd scattered as the Outdoor Girls came whirling down into its midst, but in an instant it had closed about them again. They dismounted, leaving their excited horses to go where they would, and pushed their way through to the group that seemed to be the center of all this wild demonstration.

And when they saw Meggy, fairly weeping with joy, and old Dan Higgins, holding a handful of precious golden nuggets, they nearly went mad themselves.

They kissed and hugged Meggy till she cried aloud for mercy. They kissed and hugged old Dan, and he took it as though he had been used to being made much of by pretty girls all his life.

Twenty years had fallen from the old man's age. No matter that he had wasted the best part of his life in a vain hunt for gold. His dream had been realized at last. There was a fortune in his grasp, and he felt again the thrill that had coursed through his veins when, as a young man, heart high with aspirations, he had started on his quest.

He was young again! Young! It seemed as though the sight of those golden nuggets—his own—had renewed the fires of youth.

Nimbly he sprang upon an empty powder keg and addressed his frenzied audience.

"Friends and fellow gold hunters," he yelled, and there was a roar of appreciation. "They is a few words I'd like to say afore we go back to wrestlin' some more gold outen them rocks. An' these is them. Ef I'm a happy man to-day an' a rich one, then it's all due to these four young gals here. They set me on the trail o' this new thing when I was purty near tuckered out. You all knows 'em an' loves 'em. Now give 'em a cheer. Hearty, now, hearty——"

Then arose such a roar that the Outdoor Girls' hearts swelled near to bursting and they felt the tears sting their eyes. That moment would be something to remember all their lives.

The roar gradually subsided and the miners wandered back to their own operations again, followed by scattered groups of curious onlookers. They worked with redoubled energy, with redoubled hope. Gold had been found. More gold would be found. It was a thrilling, glorious race to see who would be the next to announce good fortune.

Left to themselves, the girls crowded around Meggy, questioning her, congratulating her, demanding to know how it had all happened and when.

"My—my mouth is so dry I can hardly speak," said Meggy, quivering with nervous reaction. "I—I can't jest make up my mind that it has happened yet."

"We know," said Betty, soothingly. "You needn't tell us about it if you don't want to."

"But I do—I've got to!" cried Meggy tensely. "Why, it seems like a dream. But I'm so happy, so wildly happy——" A sob caught in her throat and she paused for a moment, then went on swiftly, the words tumbling over each other in her eagerness: "It was jest this morning that it happened, jest a little while ago. You know we have been workin' awful hard the last few days, an' I was getting worried over dad again. He was gittin' that thin an' weak an' kind o' discouraged, too. Seemed like he'd jest made up his mind that there wasn't no luck fer him nowhere's.

"Then——" she leaned forward, her eyes black as coals, her fingers clasped convulsively in front of her. "Then we uncovered it, that first little narrow vein o' gold runnin' through the rocks. I thought dad would go plumb crazy when he seen it. Honest, I was skeered for a minute, till I recollected thet joy never killed nobody.

"Then I began to be skeered fer myself. I felt so kind o' queer an' wobbly inside o' me. Then dad came runnin' out to show the other fellers what he'd found, an' seemed like they went crazy too.

"Then you come an'—an'—I guess thet's 'bout all."

The girls drew a long breath.

"All," repeated Grace, softly. "I should think it was about enough for one day!"

"An' now," said Meggy, in a small little voice, "poor old dad an' me, we're rich—rich! Think of it—Meggy an' her dad! Now I can buy a hoss like—like—Nigger, mebbe——"

"You funny girl," cried Betty, hugging her fondly. "Of course you can buy a horse—a dozen of them if you want to. But wouldn't you like anything else? Pretty clothes, a beautiful house to live in——"

"Yes," agreed Meggy, but without any special enthusiasm. "I used to think when you gals come around lookin' all pretty an' stylish in your nice clothes thet I would like to dress thet way myself ef I wasn't as poor as dirt. An' I would like to live in somethin' besides a shack an' have sheets enough to your beds so's you could change 'em every day ef you wanted to. Sure, I'd like them things.

"But a hoss——" Her voice lowered almost to a reverential pitch. "Ever sence I grew to be a long-legged gal, seems like all I've really wanted was a hoss. I s'pose," she turned dark, rather wistful eyes on the girls, "it's purty hard for you gals to understand what I'm talkin' about. You never longed fer a thing so's your heart ached till it seemed like it was dead inside of you. So you might think I was foolish to take on so 'bout only a hoss."

"We don't think you're foolish, Meggy," said Betty, gently. "We think you're wonderful, and you deserve every bit of the splendid luck that has come to you. And I expect," she finished gayly, "that you will have the most beautiful horse in all Gold Run."

Meggy's eyes lighted with joy. Then they misted suddenly as she looked at the girls.

"It's jest like dad said," she murmured. "We wouldn't 'a' had nothin' ef it hadn't been fer you girls. You don't know how we feel about you, 'cause we jest never could tell you."

The days that followed seemed like a beautiful fairy tale to the happy girls. Peter Levine had known what he was talking about when he had asserted that "gold was running wild" about the northern end of the ranch and its environs.

It was as though the finding of gold in the new Higgins' mine had been the key that unlocked the door to a steady stream of it.

Every day brought glad tidings of a new find, and, as some of these were on the ranch, Betty began to realize that the Nelson family was becoming very wealthy. They had always been well-to-do, for her father had prospered in his business, that of carpet manufacturer in Deepdale. But now it seemed that they were to know what it felt like to be really rich.

The girls realized this, and once Mollie put the new idea into words.

"This is a wonderful thing for you, Betty dear," she said soberly. "You can have about anything in the world that you want now. I—I—hope you won't forget your old friends." She said the last laughingly, but Betty was deeply hurt and showed that she was.

"If—if you ever dare say such a horrid thing to me again, Mollie Billette," she cried, half way between tears and anger, "I'll never, never forgive you! You—you—ought to know me better."

And Mollie, heartily ashamed of herself, succeeded in placating the Little Captain only after having apologized most abjectly.

Then one day something happened that amused them all mightily. They had all turned out to the gold diggings, Mrs.

Nelson, Mr. Nelson, the four girls, and Allen. Mrs. Nelson and Allen were engaged in the joyful pursuit of trying to figure out how much her profits would be, when Betty edged up to Allen and, pulling his sleeve, pointed out a man some distance from them. The latter was standing alone, and he seemed to be regarding the operations rather morosely.

"Peter Levine, by all that's holy!" murmured Allen. "Just hold tight for a minute, folks, and watch me chase him."

With an elaborately casual air, Allen sauntered over to the morose individual. The man looked up as he approached, and the scowl on his face deepened.

"Howdy," said Allen, loud enough to cause those near by to turn to look at him. "How's my old friend Levine this morning?"

"None of your business," snarled the other, with a black look. "Lay off me, do you hear?"

"Oh, yes, I hear," said Allen, loudly and cheerfully. "I'm quite exceptionally good at hearing. Shall I tell these friends of ours what Andy Rawlinson and I happened to hear the other night, beneath these very trees? Why, Levine, where are you going?" he asked with feigned surprise, as the other started to take his leave. "Don't you want to hear——"

"Shut your mouth!" snarled Peter Levine, furiously, then turned and slunk off, followed by the jeers and catcalls of the crowd.

"You shore hev got his number, boy," said one old timer, admiringly. "He loves you like the fox loves a trap."

Allen grinned boyishly. "Suits me!" he said cheerfully.

CHAPTER XXV

INNOCENT

"That was good, Allen," said Mr. Nelson appreciatively, as the young fellow rejoined the group. "You've licked him in fine shape."

"And we want to thank you for the way you have handled things for us, Allen," added Mrs. Nelson, warmly. "We might have got into all sorts of trouble if it hadn't been for you."

The young lawyer was tremendously embarrassed by this praise, though Betty was aglow with it. It was splendid to have her family so fond of Allen.

The latter noticed her silence, and under cover of the general conversation commented upon it.

"How feels the millionairess this morning?" he asked lightly, though Betty felt that there was a deeper meaning hidden behind the words.

"I'm feeling splendid," she answered, her voice vibrating with the joy of living. "Who wouldn't be—with all this?" and she waved her hand over the bustling scene.

In spite of the excitement of all these wonderful happenings, the girls, especially Betty, had thought almost constantly of the poor musician whom his neighbors called the Hermit of Gold Run.

He never came down to help Dan Higgins and Meggy any more, probably, Grace said, scared off by the bustle and confusion of the new gold boom. Meggy had mentioned casually once or twice that she still took food to the desperate man.

"If he only doesn't give himself up to the authorities before we get news from the East!" Betty, worried, exclaimed over and over again.

Then one day, along with the other letters in the mail, there arrived an important looking document from New York addressed to Allen.

The latter was out at the gold diggings at the time, and the girls fairly lassoed him, bringing him home protesting but helpless.

"I say, what's the row?" he demanded, and for answer Mollie thrust the important missive into his hand.

"Read!" she commanded dramatically. "And tell us what lies within."

Allen tore the envelope open and read the letter hastily through while the girls crowded around him and tried to read over his shoulder.

Then he jumped to his feet and waved the paper at them excitedly.

"By Jove!" he cried, "this proves that Betty was right. The man didn't kill his brother—simply injured him. He was taken to the hospital and he recovered long since. The manager says he has been trying to locate Paul Loup for weeks. He is losing a fortune every day——"

But Betty could wait no longer. She snatched the letter from him and read it through aloud while the girls gaped at her.

"Come on," she cried, reaching for her sailor hat and pushing it down on her shapely little head. "Don't stand there like wooden Indians. We've got to take this news to Paul Loup."

Bent on their joyful mission, the girls approached the lonely little cabin in the woods swiftly. As they came near they heard again that same hauntingly sweet melody that had so moved them the first time they had heard it.

Yet now that they understood the pain that prompted the rendering of that exquisite harmony, it seemed too bitterly sad to be beautiful, and their hearts ached dully in sympathy with Paul Loup's despair.

Tears were in Betty's eyes, but there was a smile on her lips, as she pushed open the door of the little shack and stood waiting on the threshold.

The musician saw her, ended the throbbing melody with a crash of discord, and gazed at her mutely. In all his tall, gaunt body only his glowing eyes seemed really alive, but in those eyes there was a welcome that gave Betty courage.

"Look!" she cried, holding out the paper to him. "This is from your manager. Read it—and see that you are innocent."

Slowly the man laid down his violin and bow, slowly he took the paper from Betty's trembling fingers. Like a man in a daze he read it through—then read it through again.

"I did not kill him—my brother," he murmured aloud. "My brother—that I love—I did not kill him. He is alive—he is well. *Mon Dieu*, then I am free! Paul Loup—he is not a murderer—a hunted thing. He is again the artist—free— *free*—" His voice, which had been gradually rising as the truth bore in upon him, rose to a jubilant shout and he threw out his arms passionately as though to encompass them all in his newly found love of life. "The world——" he said brokenly, "the world is very beautiful!"

Silently the girls rode through the sunshine and shadow-filled forest, their hearts filled with a happiness so poignant it seemed almost pain.

"What a wonderful, wonderful summer!" breathed Mollie. "I don't believe we have ever had one like it, girls."

"I wish we didn't have to go home," sighed Amy. "I shall miss my beautiful Lady so," and she laid a loving hand on the little animal's arching neck.

"What about me?" wailed Grace. "I know I shall cry myself to sleep, longing for Nabob. He's one of the best chums I ever had."

But the Little Captain did not hear them. Over and over again, like an echo, her mind was repeating those words of Paul Loup: "The world is very beautiful."

"Girls," she murmured dreamily, "everybody is so happy—and I'm so happy—oh, please, don't wake me up—anybody!"

And so, at the end of a wonderful outing, with life stretching gloriously before them, we will once more sadly, reluctantly, wave farewell to the Outdoor Girls.

The End